T0063069

His Story
in the Skies

M. J. Swanson

WESTBOW°
PRESS
A DIVISION OF THOMAS NELSON
& ZONDERVAN

WestBow Press books may be ordered through booksellers or by contacting:

WestBow Press
A Division of Thomas Nelson & Zondervan
1663 Liberty Drive
Bloomington, IN 47403
www.westbowpress.com
1 (866) 928-1240

ISBN: 978-1-4908-4154-0 (sc)
ISBN: 978-1-4908-4153-3 (e)

Library of Congress Control Number: 2014913175

Printed in the United States of America.

WestBow Press rev. date: 11/25/2014

Contents

Preface and purpose

1) To preserve extant prophesies logged by our antediluvian ancestors prior to the flood; to clear-cut through many of the corruptions of these prophesies that began in Babel in the times of Nimrod—Cir. 2100 BC, that resulted in astrology, myths, idolatry, etc. culminating in God's poetic judgment on man confusing man's language.

2) Additionally the certain fact that after the millennial reign of Christ on this earth comes to a close, (Thy kingdom come) and all things are accomplished according to scripture and prophesy, God will make a new heaven and earth...
...for this reason to get it back to the original intent (sans myths) seems worth the effort, and in retrospect we have for ourselves a sure foundation in His Word should the story seem to stray by misinterpretations.

3) It's beneficial to understand the intent of the story in the sky, *even as it still refers to biblical events to come.* By this fact they are still relevant to us at this writing, (and possibly for an historical document for future ages) complementing scripture, a separate though somewhat broken witness there confirmed by the Eternal Word, in visions; visions displayed for the most part, an ancient foreshadowing of the New Testament

<Cover illustration- Deli, The water pourer>

'It is good that a man should both hope and quietly wait for the salvation of the LORD.' Lamentations 3:26 6th century BC

Part 1

General scientific overview

For clarity and familiarity the Latin names of the signs are used here. In chapter 4 some of the original Semitic names will be introduced.

Like clockwork

"And God said, let there be lights in the firmament of the heaven to divide the day from the night; and let them be for signs, and for seasons, and for days, and years: ...and let them be for lights in the firmament of the heaven to give light upon the earth: and it was so." Gen.1:14.

'.....for seasons, and for days, and years:'

The moon's cycle or orbit determined the length of the 'month' orbiting the earth roughly 12-1/3 times in a solar year at approximately 29.531 day intervals. Some modern nations still use a lunar calendar to measure the months, seasons, and years; which set their months on the cycle of the moon. These nations require the addition of a 'leap' month or corrective month every few years to keep them intact with the solar year;-sidereal, or tropical.

Their months and years do not align easily with the Julian calendar, which attempts to align fixed periods of time (*still called months, originally based on the cycle of the moon*) by the position of the sun instead of the moon. Two measurements oftime are called-

1) *The Tropical year*, marked by the Solstice and Equinox, which divide the 4 seasons; and...
2) *The Sidereal year*, by the position of a star/ grouping completing an apparent cycle around the earth to a fixed point - 12 constellations fixed, 12 divisions of time per year...The year was then determined to be 365.24 days. (65 BC)

The Seasons

(Based on observances from northern latitudes). The earth's rotation on its axis is what changes the seasons as we know, tilting northward (upward) in its orbit around the sun in what we call autumn and winter and downward in spring and summer. The seasons are marked by astronomical observances, the equinox and solstice.

(All caused by the earth's fluctuating rotation during the course of a year)

Celestial equator

In the earth's orbital plane around the sun, the earth's axis wobbles like a top up, down. The projected plane of this varying equator is called the celestial equator. It is varied from the solar ecliptic which is stationary across The 12 primary constellations. When that plane lines with the center of the sun, (crosses the sun's ecliptic plane) it is called...

The Equinox

The equinox is the point where the sun meets our equator on its *apparent* journey southward and northward. These points mark the start of autumn on its journey southward around the 23rd of September called the Autumnal equinox: And spring on its journey northward around the 21st of March called the Vernal equinox.

The Solstice

The solstice is when the sun reaches its highest point (northernmost ecliptic path) and marks the beginning of summer around the 21st of the month June, where the sun reaches vertical over the tropic of Cancer: And conversely its lowest point the 22nd of December vertical over the tropic of Capricorn beginning winter.

The 21st of June is thereby referred to as the longest day of the year, Summer solstice..... And December 22nd the shortest day, Winter solstice in regard to the amount of time the sun remains visible *in the northern latitudes* during a day's length.

The Solar ecliptic line = Earth's orbital plane around the sun

The 12 primary signs are set on the suns' ecliptic line (earth's orbital plane around the sun) so that at any given time the sun is eclipsing through one of them, (in front of) between the signs and earth. At that point in time the stars of that sign are not visible here on earth being obscured by the sun. The sun's ecliptic is directly linked to the line of the earth's orbit around the sun and is considered the same plane.

Precession of the Equinox

Up until around 150 BC the sidereal year measured by stars, and the tropical year measured by seasons; (see seasons, months and years) were thought to be the same length. However the sidereal was then calculated to be 1.0000385 tropical years. This amounted to movement of approximately 1 degree of 360, or 1 day in a year worth of distance in every 71 years. Roughly one 12th or one full constellation or Mazzeroth in 2133 years. This means that the position of the sun at *the Vernal equinox* in relation to the constellations has shifted over the last 6000 years from and through Taurus, then Aries, and now near the end of Pisces, *and will be in Aquarius.* And simultaneously the *Autumnal equinox* is situated nearing the end of its course through the constellation Virgo around the 21st of September, whereas it was in Scorpio 6000 years ago, and finishing through Libra around the times of Christ. *The Autumnal equinox will be in Leo next.*

There is a northward precession as well as the left to right precession of the equinox discussed above. The northward shift has been attributed to gravitational forces.The Southern Cross used to be visible in northern latitudes until approx. 2000 years ago, and the pole star, or closest to the North Pole axis of the earth changed from Thuban in Draco, to Polaris in Ursa Minor.

Rough Edges

Variations in names and starts of seasons in the west occurred during the Roman republic, when it transitioned toward empire. The names of July (Julius), and August (Augustus) named from Julius Caesar and Augustus Caesar were inserted after June. Janus, and Februs... January and February were inserted before March replacing Quintillius (causing the names September through December to be 2months out of sync with their definition-7th -10th), as the new year was brought back 2 months from March, (ides of March) to January. Along with this the extra month every 3rd, or 4th year known as Mensis was eliminated, and10 days were thereby added to each year from355to 365... The year was calculated to be 365.24 days in 65 BC, therefore a leap year every fourth year adding a day to the year, to 366...The formation of the Julian calendar was said to be complete in 46 BC.

The Hebrew New Year starts in September, (autumn), as do their days start at dusk or evening, holding to the biblical standard -"And the evening and morning were the first day..." Gen.1: 5, carrying prophetic significance to their days and seasons.The Byzantines used Sept 1st as their new year,; Alexandrians (of Egypt) Aug. 30th.

Pope Gregory in 1582 reformed the Julian calendar saying 10 days needed to be dropped to realign the calendar with the seasons, Oct 5th became Oct 15th and so on.

Time is dictated by the creation, man can only attempt to measure periods accurately. Since the beginning as earlier noted, times and seasons were marked by solar, lunar and other astronomical events as was ordained by God in

Genesis. Our calendar being divided into 12 months, ajar from the original times set by astronomical marks can be difficult to follow. Perhaps things of this nature were the purpose behind the errors of Babel;....i.e.... to confuse to such a degree as to sever the noticeable link between the Creator's perfect symmetry in his creation, and our association with this witness. Whether intentional or not, the witness remains in spite of man.

Another error that is known to astronomers, and hid from most astrologers is that the movement caused by the precession has misaligned the very zodiac by more than one full sign which astrologers call the 'birth' sign. If one fashions his or herself as a 'Libra' for example, in reality they were born when the sun was in Virgo. So even astrologers are misled based on lack of knowledge of astronomy, even as they mislead others.

Part 2

Origin and intent

Origins

The prophetic interpretation and division of the 48 original constellations are antediluvian (prior to the flood) Genesis1.

The original 48 signs are perfectly placed and named in order and sequence in such a way as you will see, they are beyond mans own invention. They will be shown as prophesy, due to the translated names of the signs; and as stars they are by no means random.

'*He tells the number of the stars; He calls them all by their names.*' *(Psalm 147:4)* Therefore those names which remain from the most remote times were logged down by antediluvian *prophets*, akin to Adam; Seth's family through Enoch... that it was those Godly men which began 'calling on the name of the Lord'. This happened in Seth's time. He was the son who replaced Abel who was killed by Cain.

"*...Seth, to him also there was born a son, Enos: then began men to call upon the name of the LORD.*" *Gen. 4:26*

Seth's descendants lived happy lives in antediluvian times and were also the compilers and... '*inventors of that peculiar wisdom which is concerned with the heavenly bodies and their order*', the science known as astronomy. *(Flavius Josephus, Antiquities of the Jews)*

Josephus the Jewish historian of the 1st century AD elaborates the general history of the origin and preservation of the 48 signs which (Seth's descendants) logged down and preserved one in stone and one in brick -monuments, so to survive the catastrophic flood foretold to come on the earth, and the monument survived in Josephus' day and was then to be '*found in the land of 'Siriad.*' *(Egypt).* (see Flavius Josephus' Antiquities of the Jews book 1 Ch 2; Paragraph 3). It is somehow equated with the Great pyramids of Giza, one once having engravings of both history, and astronomy, and the other having medical discoveries. Both written in the original language before Babel. Sometime during the Moslem conquests those treasures were lost, destroyed, or hidden.

The Egyptians also claim a remote ancestor named 'Set', or Seti 1. This is likely the same as Seth, considering the findings in their land. Egypt was known early by its northern neighbors as the land of Ham, and these were known to be interested in astronomy.

Postdiluvian ancestors of Shem's son Arphaxad, the Chaldeans, Heb. translated to Kassdiyah, Kasdiy, -also called Kassites, became renowned astronomers of their times, and taught, or re-taught the Egyptians. Josephus states that Abram also revealed to them (Egypt) a closer interpretation to the original.

From Egypt the Greeks were taught, and from Babylon others went, and the message seemed to get hidden behind the confluence of myths in between. Stories were invented regarding the constellations as though they had taken place in the past, but they actually referred to things to come.

Just as it is impossible for man to create and arrange the stars in heaven; so is it impossible for fallen man to correctly name them in their prophetic significance, without knowing the One who made them. That took the walk of the prophets of old. Seth, Enoch before Noah, as an example, walked with God and God (transferred him without dying).

"For God is not the author of confusion, but of Peace." 1 Corinthians 14:33

The 48 signs are prophetic pictures. Many modern myths associated with them unwittingly contain buried reflections of the original intent, showing an ancient understanding of their original meaning which then became mutated after Babel. The principalities of Babel still exist today in the movements of unity (without God), IE 'imagine no heaven, above us only sky...' This is Babylon's 'dream', and this is what Babylon was all about, vying for domination, control over man, apart from God—God's Word. The formation of the prophetic story is not tied to Babel, however the myths and misconceptions tied to them by many ancient peoples can be traced there, and from there its' influence is shown in these days with the modern astronomical union adding many 'new' constellations having no connection to the meaning of the 48 original.

Just as a story can be told over and over and gets changed in the process over time through misunderstanding or misinterpretation, so did this important prophetic story of things to come become misunderstood or corrupted over time, that when the events of the story began taking place, only a handful were left who seemed to understand the prophetic significance....most notably, the wise men from the east at Jesus's birth. The myths were the result of the infection of Babel (confusion) in the days of Nimrod when the rebellion began. The system of Babel still seems bent on destroying, or severing the perception and understanding of this witness from man. If one's life depended on knowing the story, the hope attached to it, the promise associated with it, and one came along and began to change the meaning of the story........it would be a serious misleading ; by confusing the hope and promise of redemption to come in favor of man-made myths and idols and arrogance. Consider the damage this system can wreak on an individual, let alone nation in misleading away from truth alone...

In poetic justice similar, God confounded their single language into many at the Tower of Babel. And consider this as to why God hates Idolatry, mocks astrology, and forecast Babylon's judgment.

Around Babylon the mixed people who spoke the same language seem to have begun fiction. Creating myths and tales like Hollywood fantasies around the fixed antediluvian prophecies connected to the stars, mixing up God's creative witness, they built a tower, *and attempted to rewrite prophecy into their own likings* and it was there that God confused *their* language, scattering them over the whole earth.

So where there was originally conformity, with a single language now the story is told and completed in differing languages, yet the story is/was one, and remains one story.

What then are the Pictures?

Visions, symbolic characters, dreams, via messengers etc., are some of God's unique way of communicating that expand and clarify His Word; of events, or things, and in many cases are incorporated into His written Word, coming from the Word Himself. They elaborate character or intensity, color the event as only God can. Trying to completely understand the varieties would be near impossible as trying to understand all God's ways simultaneously. The books of the bible are filled with visions, symbolic dreams, and revelations, and the revelation to mankind continues in dreams, prophecies, visions, etc. through the living church through these times as well.

The naming and arrangement of the constellations are some of the earliest complete series of prophetic visions which are found. Earlier than Ezekiel's visions, earlier than Daniels visions of the latter times, earlier than John's Revelation. The differences between these prophets and the visions fixed on the sky, is then the ones are written in books by Hebrew prophets in Hebrew, translated into a variety of languages; and the other on the sky in an ancient language, I call Noetic—..The original language before the tower of Babel, and the interpreters were more apt to make mistakes on the latter after the confusion of languages at Babel.

The signs in the sky are like a supporting cast to the revelation of scripture, which has been there since the beginning. They are pictures illustrating the written revelation of God's Word, specifically, the New Testament....yet this witness in creation is held in place itself BY the Word. Visions fixed on the sky from the foundation (creation) of the world. Visions positioned in such a manner that the world spins on its axis to view them once a day. God speaks to Job of them, the wise men from the east found Jesus by their signal. Josephus the historian of the first century AD writes that Abraham was familiar with their meaning and taught the Egyptians much of these things; (the Egyptian Coptic's took readily to the Good News even to this day under persecution.)

Joel the prophet writes in his book the prophesy that God would reveal *wonders in the Heavens* in the last days; and Peter on the day of Pentecost confirmed that we were entering the latter times in history, by quoting Joel's prophesy under the anointing of the Holy Spirit.

How do we know what they mean?

So that we realize they are antediluvian visions first, is one part, the other part is the interpretation, what they mean or represent, which also God was to reveal through his prophets. God named all the stars.

He revealed names of many stars to his prophets of old and the names themselves when translated, interpret the visions.

As mentioned earlier, the names were originally logged in the language of those days, Noetic, which is akin to the Semitic branch of languages. From this sprang the modern Aleph-Beth, Alphabet (a), derived from the original language. In order to attempt to interpret the undefined Noetic names an understanding of the meaning of letters is required. According to a book published in 1999 by Marc Alain Oaknin titled Mysteries of the Alphabet, the ancient meanings of letters are revealed. Pictographs were a primitive form of letters, and they morphed into letters. Many of us have seen the charts of proto-languages forming over time into something resembling our own today. This is not an attempt to show the progression of the language from pictograph into letters, but to take the foundational meaning of the original letter and to combine it with the others to form the definition of a word unknown.

(I will introduce the general definitions of the letters as laid out in Oaknin's book separately, before the constellations are listed in this book).

These wonders are the New Testament in the sky written in old times... as God has given us pictures to coincide the story of his redemption plan: which was foretold in antediluvian days. However, their literal fulfillment only began being manifest on earth around the times near to Christ's birth; starting with the Virgin, which represented those waiting for the Promise to come in Israel, the news of the forthcoming birth of the Messiah; in Israel itself,

which had fallen at that time under Roman rule, as the Virgin is shown as having fallen.

This particular point in time is (like clockwork) marked by the visit of the angel Gabriel, and the simultaneous journey of the wise men from the east toward Jerusalem, beginning the story from Virgo around its decans (see below). And onward to today.

Roughly two thirds of the story is fulfilled, and we are (at this writing) at the final third portion, with Taurus turning east (the Judge, Judgment coming); and will be completing at Leo, (the vehemently Returning One).

Another layer to be researched in the future...

Wonders that have been revealed recently in this generation are the nebulae. Wonderful explosions of light and color, smoke and fire positioned in the story line in such a way that they upon further study are *to be found prophetic themselves* ...being detailed, and graphic. Look at God's artwork photographed from space. These starbursts, explosions of gasses and dust and color are seen by high powered telescopes such as the Hubble space telescope in all their color and clarity, and are wonders so to speak, even as stated by Joel, and reiterated by Peter, that...

'..... *it shall come to pass afterward, that I will pour out my Spirit upon all flesh; and your sons and daughters shall prophesy, your old men will dream dreams, your young men will see visions: And also upon the servants and upon the handmaids in those days will I pour out my Spirit. And I will show (reveal, display) wonders in the heavens and in the earth, blood, and fire, and pillars of smoke. The sun shall be turned into darkness, and the moon into blood, before the great and the terrible day of the Lord come. And it shall come to pass, that whosoever shall call upon the name of the Lord shall be delivered: for in mount Zion and in Jerusalem, shall be deliverance, as the Lord has said, and in the remnant whom the Lord will call.'*

Joel 2:28-31 cir.800 BC

Part 3

Language of the ancients

Marc Alain Oaknin's *Mysteries of the Alphabet*, published 1999 lists the letters and histories of the dispensation of the alphabet from its origins, its meaning, and each individual letter. It can be called Paleo-Hebrew, or Noetic, since it seems to be the language understood prior to Babel.

With this tool you can yourself learn the meaning of any word written in the alpha-beta format, which covers a large part of the globe- with the help of the Holy Spirit.

Here is the way to read what we have handed to us from ancient times.

Every letter of the Semitic, later Phoenician, Sanskrit, Greek, etc. thereafter all nations which use a form of the Alphabet, or Aleph-Beth not using (Hieroglyphs) *has a distinct meaning or representation.*

So then the Semitic language (Hebrew, Arabic, Aramaic, etc.) works the best with this layout usually holding to the original, followed by the gentiles which also use a form of the alphabet from the (Greek, Aryan, Cyrillic or Etruscan- Latin, possibly Runic) basics. All are based on the foundation of the Noetic original, whether borrowed from one another or from the original. In order for these names to be referred to as legitimate, the old names must bear out the story independently. And they do. Independent of the present religious views or conditions of the naming nations.

The hieroglyphs, the cuneiform, these seem to be unrelated to the Aleph-Beth, yet their origins are also developed from symbols in antiquity. Modern pictographs, condensed Asian characters with meanings from old times may be holdovers from the days of hieroglyphs. Having meaning in themselves, they are for the user adequate. Yet to begin to understand the meanings of the ancient language, they must be someway converted into the Aleph -Beth.

Therefore the nations which did not use a form of the Alphabet were hard-pressed to interpret correctly the original meaning of the story, and were compelled to make their own maps in their own ideas. Some countries kept a close watch on the sky, and accurately applied the science of astronomy; nonetheless changed the groupings considerably to be unrecognizable to the middle-east and some western nations, which in contrast kept the signs rather uniform, even with some language barriers. Those eastern nations carrying with them the numerous pictographs developed into what it is today, the characters of the Chinese and other Asian nation's languages. However, China kept a few names of stars which were lost in the west, and many of them fit perfectly into the story, proving a common understanding by all people at one point in history.

Oaknin's book details the history behind these letters, and is a good read on this subject.

The letters

The letter first, -The Greek, Hebrew designation second- symbolic origin third, the meaning and general interpretation fourth.

The letters carry a literal, figurative, and symbolic meaning. Most of the definitions are in the figurative...as 'm' does not mean a literal river on a map in every word it is included into, but most often speaks of an 'outpouring', and such. This is the way it is arranged...Starting with...

A, α-A, a -Alpha
א-Aleph-an Ox- powerful, strength, authority, mighty, to lead, start

B, β-B, b-Beta
ב- Beth—a House- body, home, place, residence, domain, where you live, your location

Γ, γ-C, c- Gamma
ג-Gimmel-a Camel- breaking out, deliverance, action of deliverance, action of freeing

Δ, δ-D, d-Delta
ד-Daleth—a Door—weaned, set freed, past tense freed, liberated, independent

E, ε-E, e-Epsilon
ה- Heh—Air—breath, prayer, life, air, blood

Y, υ-F, f- U, u -V, v, -W, w—Upsilon
ו, וו-Vav—a Nail—union, link, connection, fixed as with a nail, W doubly fixed, connected or allied. Crux (anciently the Greeks assigned the number six to a now obsolete

letter 'stigma' which remains only in the lower case letter of the final form of 'sigma')

Z, ζ-G, g Z, z-Zeta
ז-Zayin —an Arrow—weapon, confrontation, warring, shoot, shot, attack

H, η-H, h, Ch-Eta
ח-Cheth—an Enclosure—captive, barrier, separated, imprisoned (as penalty, punishment)

Θ, θ-Th, th-Theta
ט-Teth—a Shield—guarded, protected, attack repelled

I, ι-I i, J j, Yy-Iota
י, ״-Yod—a Hand extended—reaching, extended, helping

K, κ-K, k-Kappa
ך, כ-Kaf or Caph—a Palm of hand—hold, own, have, receive, retain

Λ, λ-L, l-Lambda
ל-Lamed—an Ox goad, or prod—teaching, instruct, learn, prompt

M, μ-M, m-Mu
מ, ם- Mem—a Stream -as Water—flowing out, forth... pouring out

N, ν-N,n-Nu,
נ, ן-Nun—a Game fish—hidden life, to multiply, perpetual, seed, offspring, perpetuate

Ξ, ξ-X, x-Xi
ס-Samekh—a Tree—framework, structure, support, lean on

O, o-O, o-Omicron
ע-Ayin—an Eye—to see, perceive, vision, envision, spiritual insights, literal and figurative

Π, π-P, p-Pi
פ,ף- Peh—a Mouth—speech, words, talking, Word

M, м-Archaic Ts, Tz, Cz-San
צ, ץ-Tsadeh—a Fishhook—a snare, hunted, caught, pulled out

Q, q- Archaic Q, q-, Q or (K) oppa
ק-Qoph—an Ape—limited, stubborn, difficult

P, ρ-R, r—Rho
ר-Resh—A Head—Beginning, chief, Lord, king, primary

Σ, σ, ς-S, s-Sigma
ש-Shin—a Tooth—bite, sharp, crush, devour

T, τ-T, t-Tau
ת-Tav—a Sign—a mark, sign, finishing, or completion
Archaic Greek letters, no longer commonly used in Greek, yet passed onto other scripts

Φ, φ-Phi; X, x-Chi; Ψ,ψ-Psi; and Ω, ω-Omega

Sampi- written like a diagonal comb pronounced like 'TS, KS, or S'

Wau-now upsilon pronounced like 'W' written like 'F'. See Hebrew Vav.

Heta (now eta) pronounced like 'H' written like sideways 'T'. See Hebrew Chet.

Yot (now iota) pronounced like a ' j ' written like a ' j '. See Hebrew Yod

Qoppa-dropped for the most part) pronounced like a 'K' written like a'Q', same as Hebrew Qoph.

Stigma-now small case final sigma pronounced like 'ST', written lower case ς.

These Greek discontinued letters originated from an alphabet similar to the Hebrew. The ancient Greek alphabet found on Crete from 800 BC was written from right to left same as the Semitic languages, and was identical to Semitic save in the design with 2 letters phei, and chei, added. (phi, and chi). The right to left writing was the norm in those days and may show the original searching of the skies from right to left from the northern latitudes. The Greek historians state they learned their language from the original inhabitants of the area. These were the Pelasgians, which were likely a Semitic nation living in the eastern Mediterranean.

Testing the theory

Using the letter definitions just described you can test the validity of the system with the name for one constellation -Crux; or, the southern cross. If you take the 4 letters back to their original meaning, you get C-Deliverer (ing)(ed) R-Head, Chief, Lord U-Fixed, attached (as with a nail) X-Framework-structure, support..(originally tree)

There you have the crucifixion explained since remote times all contained in the word CRUX.

Another example.

The old name for Bootes was Bo, which simply means physically, or bodily seen, or observed.. B- Physically O -Seen.

And for this sign the Arabs had the title Al Awwa, (Al-The, Awwa-Pastor, the Shepherd. Lit-the Annointed.) The Hebrews knew it was 'the Coming One...'

The Arabic designation Al which is translated here generally as the prefix 'The'...is broken down to The Leader teaches..,or strength from knowing, the primary teacher, -primary knowledge, foundational..

This translation can be used on any form of the Aleph-Beth, Alpha- Beta. This is due to the fact the Alpha-Bet is derived from ancient Semitic letters, re-distributed by Semitic peoples.

The Phoenicians at a point in history (mid 2nd millennium BC) change their writing method from Hieroglyphs, to the Phoenician Alpha-bet. Phoenecian later on was considered a Semitic language, though they are originally of Canaanite decent. The Arameans, and Arabians also spread the Semitic language throughout the Middle East...as did the Lydians, and Arphaxadites of Crete for the Greeks, and Etruscans (from Lydia, - Lud a son of Shem) for the Latins. Runic letters also are proving to have been widespread from the Scythian-Indo-Europeans of Eurasia, reaching the northern parts of Eurasia. Another discovery is whenever the Chinese language is translated from their characters into the Alpha-bet, then the same principle for translation is in effect using the Semitic origins as well.

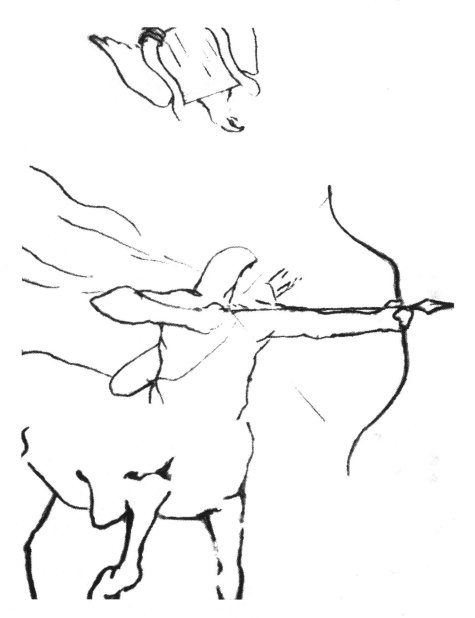

Kesheth, Hebrew
Ashada, Hindi

Part 4

The Signs

Mazzeroth-Overview-48 original signs

The constellations are as at ancient times divided into 48 original.

No point is necessary to try to understand the modern additions by the astronomical union, which incorporated many new signs that do not fit the original story.

The original 48 signs are set in sequence by the 12 divisions of the primary signs known anciently as '*mazzeroth*', also as '*the way*', we know them as *zodiac; (*from *zoad, a walk, way or going by steps).

(Not to be confused with astrology -the misuse of the signs for money, profit, manipulation, deceit)

Decans

The 12 primary signs are each supported by 3 signs, significant to the theme of the event logged by the primary sign. These supporting signs are called 'decans', Semitic 'dek' piece or part. This is where the term dec, for 10 came up. These supporting signs are set perfectly in place, carrying with them a deeper commentary into the theme of the main sign. These decans are found within or near the 30 degrees (of 360) that are apportioned to the primary sign.

Interpretations

There are 3 basic levels of interpretation, or definitions of the figures or asterisms.

The first and most basic is a *Figure Identity Location* definition, IE 'the knee' of the figure, or 'the shoulder of the......' These are for the location and specifics of the physical attributes of the figure. (loc.)

The second would be the *Traditional definition* ...IE 'the Coming One', or 'the Victorious'...what the asterism or figure represents. These contain some of the old root meanings, and characteristics. Usually the traditional definition is a condensed version of the third type. (tr.), or (trad.)

The third would be the translation from the original Noetic -Semitic- roots into an even more precise, and defined translation. I will refer to this as the *Literal definition*. *This is the one that can cross check the Traditional, or the Figure Identity Location definition, if necessary, due to a missing definition, or one seeming to be out of place with the story.* (lit.)

All three definitions are important and combined can expand the vision with an interpretation, thereby confirming it.

The literal definitions I postulate in this book are my best attempt at defining the names which either I do not have, or I wanted to clarify. They are by no means absolutely complete or fully expounding on the story. This is only a reflection of the story that was written by the prophets inspired by the Holy Spirit in the Word, but a reminder of His promises from ages past to all nations.

Remember that this is just scratching the surface.

The antediluvian line to Noah lived hundreds of years, taking advantage of their prolonged years to perfect their study in the earliest times. What I'm doing here is digging out much of this as mining ore so to speak, yet it is rough ore and needs continued purification. So the rough ore is brought out to see. It would take many books and many years to completely perfect and clarify every asterism involved or known, and as I stated in 'another layer to be researched…' at the end of part 2, there is another level further in this story which I am about certain will detail further the story in what we call the nebulaei, and these may likely be the wonders in the heavens which Peter and Joel spoke of. Blood, fire, and pillars of smoke.

You may find that few, (very few) of the names are either undefined, or you may want to clarify them further in the literal translation, and it is possible to define them with the tools put forth in this book.

As well the reader may need a sky map as a co-reference to this book. You need as well a bible with a concordance. It will aid in your understanding of the names and prophetic locations of this witness.

The prophetic story piece by piece comes to life in an ancient foretelling of the Gospel millennia before the times of Christ.

Mankind has always had this witness, and the witness is relevant today, as some of the story in the sky is yet to come to pass.This is the Love of God, the Promise of God to a generation we are largely unaware of…the antediluvian race which we aare all descended. All of mankind descended from faithful men, believers in the Creator. This story was compiled by those early believers to which only the architect Himself would reveal.

'The Heavens declare the Glory of God; and the firmament shows his handiwork. Day unto day utters speech, and night unto night shows knowledge. There is no speech nor language, where their voice is not heard.

Their line is gone out through all the earth, and their words to the end of the world. In them has He set a tabernacle for the sun, Which is as a bridegroom coming out of his chamber, and rejoices as a strong man to run a race. His going forth is from the end of heaven, and his circuit unto the ends of it: and there is nothing hid from the heat thereof.' Psalm 19:1-6

Bethulah, Hebrew/ Latin-Virgo

Bethulah, Hebrew...*a virgin*
Bethalto, Syriac...*virgin*
Al Adhara Al Nathifa, Arabic...*the innocent, the maiden*
Aspolia, Coptic...*station of the desired*
Kanya, Canya, India...*young girl gains*...later post Alexander
Partina, Parthena, India...*virgin*—from Greek
Parthenos, Greek...*virgin*
Virgo, Latin....*virgin*
Maeden, Anglo-Saxon...*maid*
Dufhiza Dakhiza, Turcoman...*pure virgin*
Sha-Niu, Chinese...*house of the virgin*
Virgine, Italian/ Vierge, French/ Junfrau, German...*virgin*
Kauni, Tamil...*the fertile*
Khosa, Khuzak, Persian...*prophetess*

Alpha   1.3 (magnitude) white   in left hand of virgin

Al Simak- Arabic...*the defenseless, the unarmed.*
Al Azal, Arabic...lit. *start of the Words' powerful knowledge*
Shibboleth, Hebrew... ear *of wheat.*
Spica, Spigha, Spicum, Spike, l'epi, Indo-European...*grain of wheat*
Virgin's Spike, Old English... (*of wheat)*

Keok, Guik, Chinese... *star of spring, later* -Kio, *spike, or horn*

Repa, Egyptian...*the Lord*. Aratos said this is *"in her hands"*

Citra, Hindu... *bright, Lamp, pearl*

Salkim, Turkish...*cluster of grapes...overwhelming yield... abundance*

Shibbelta, Syrian, Aramaic...*Promised Victor, (Messiah)*

Beta 3.9   pale yellow   *by left ear of virgin

Zavijava, Latin...and Arabic, Al Zawiah...*the beautiful, glorious...*

Mashaha, Persian..... Fastashat, Sogdian...Afsasat, Khorasmian

(*all with the same designation as Arabic*).

Yew Chi Fa, Chinese...*the Right Hand maintainer of law.*

Abukia, Coptic...*future help*

*If by the ear it suggests something heard.

Gamma   3, 3.2 white binary (2)   between
left arm and left side of virgin

Porrima, or antevorta and postvorta, Latin.... *prophetesses*

Zawiat al Awwa, Arabic....*the turning of the corner*. lit. - (theta or tau). *Word of the Messiah*

Shang Seang, Chinese...*High Minister of state.*

Delta 3.6   golden yellow   on her belly

Min Al Awwa, Arabic...lit. *Advent of the Great Shepherd... Messiah*

Mina Lauva, Latin... *the unseen Shepherd*

Lu Lim, Euphratian - Akkadian...*the King*

Tsze Seang, Chinese...*the second Minister of state*

Epsilon   3.3 bright yellow   on right
forearm holding the branch

Vindemiator, Indo-European, from the old Noetic. ...
Divine Mediator, vindicator in its root form.
Vindemiatrix,...variation of above, *Divine vindicator,
indicating 3 fold...(triune?)....*
Euphrates name ...*'Divine King of (in) the desert- Man of
fire..'*
Al Muridin, Arabic...*The sent forth; who shall come down.
The Living Liberator
Tsze Tseang, Chinese...*the Second General.*
Mukdim al Kitaf, Arabic...lit. *Liberator given*

Eta   3-4 variable   on left shoulder of virgin

Al Zawiah, Arabic...*the corner - trad.*
Tso Chih Fa, Chinese.....*the left-hand maintainer of law.*
Heze, (old Noetic)...*intersession*

Theta   4.4, 9, &10 triple...pale white,
violet, and dusky.   left thigh, side

Apima Atsa, Indus...*child of the waters.*
Ping Taou, Chinese...*the plain and even way.*

Iota   4.2   on skirt or garment low by feet

Al Ghafr, Arabic....*the covering.*
Syrma, Greek...*garment train.*

Sigma, and Tau

Tien Teen, Chinese...*the heavenly fields; (sigma, and tau) (in the branch)*
Al Azal, Arabic........*the Branch*

This sign represents the congregation Israel as having fallen, but given a great hope, who ministers to this fallen virgin, the advent, calling, and earthly ministry of Christ.

Subilah Coma—Decan of Bethulah.

Subilah Coma, Hebrew... *who bears the desired.*
Adara, Arabic... *virgin separated, (as in chambers)*

Individual star names cannot be located with certainty for this constellation, though groupings are known, and named.

Coma, Hebrew...*the Desired*
Al Awa, Arabic...*the Desired -The beginning*
Al Eced, Arabic....*the united, the birth*
Adrenosa, Arabic roots...*persecution forewarned*
Haza-Methon, or Al Huzmat, Arabic....*pile of grain*
Al Haud, Arabic...*the pond*
Shes-Nu, Egypt...*the desired Son -*
Prometheus, Greek...*Deliverer- root meaning God's Promised One.*

'It has been suggested by Lanseer, Sabaean Researches, p.186 from the study of an Assyrian symbolic monument, that the stars which Conon converted into the Coma Berenices-....and which lie in Leo opposite the Pleiades in Taurus, were originally constellated as a Dove....' 'Star names- Their Lore and Meaning.' P.170 R. H. Allen. Dover publishers.

The above observation of Anc. Assyrian astronomical symbols placing a Dove where Coma is today fits well just above (as carrying) the Branch into the right hand of the Virgin...........and the Egyptians denoted a seated woman holding a child at Coma so if you transpose the Assyrian Dove over the Egyptian Virgin seated....you have a prophetic picture of what happened. Mary was overshadowed by the Spirit of God, symbolically and literally bringing the Branch. This antediluvian sign was forecast in type when Noah sought land and sent out the dove which brought him back an olive branch, and when the Holy Spirit was seen in bodily form as a dove coming to rest on Jesus (the *Branch), literally bringing the Branch to us. *See Zechariah 3:8

*Albumazer said; "There arises in the first decan, as the Persians, Chaldeans, and Egyptians, and the two Hermes, and Ascalius, teach, a young woman, whose Persian name denotes a pure virgin, sitting on a throne, nourishing an

infant boy, said boy having a Hebrew name, by some nations called Ihesu, with the signification Iesa, which in Greek is called Christ.'

(Albumazer was an Arab astronomer of the Caliphs of Grenada, Spain about 900 AD. Also called Abu Masher)

*The Gospel in the Stars. Kregel publications p.28,29 Joseph A Seiss author.

In the Dresden globe, a distaff is held in the virgin's hand. A distaff was (is) a cleft stick for holding fiber in spinning thread- *The distaff side is for the female line in weaving and spinning.*

The Chinese took great interest in this grouping, and noted the new bright star in the area of the infant's head of Coma 2 millennia ago. This new star was so bright as to be seen in the daytime around the times just before the birth of Christ; yet had faded soon afterwards...see Gospel in the Stars, Joseph A. Seiss, Kregel publications. See Gen. 3: 15

The seed of the woman; Christ is born

Bootes—Decan of Bethulah

Bo, Hebrew....tr. ...*the Coming One*. lit.... *bodily, or physically seen..*
Bootes, Noetic, Hebrew...*Driver, Good Shepherd (guardian) Physically seen.*
Boote, Italian, Greek...*Driver of the Wain*
Bouvier, French...*Herdsman*
Vociferator, Syntaxis 'translation of'...*Shouter*
Al Awwa, Arabic....*Shepherd, Herdsman of the nearby fold*. In the Noetic sense means *Annointed" (Messiah)*
Pastor, Arabic....*the Shepherd*
Pastinator, Hydes' translation of Arabic...*Leader of Pastures, Builder of...*
Vintager, *digger, trencher of a vinyard*
Rising in the morning twilight coincides with the Autumn Equinox at the time of the grape harvest.

Alpha   .3 golden yellow   on knee

Arcturus, Greek....*Guardian of Arctos (the little flock)*
Arctur, German...Arturo, Spanish and Italian...Arthur, English...same as Greek
Svati, Indus...*Good Goer.*
Ta Kio, Chinese...*the Great Horn (leader)*

Al Haris Al Sama, Arabic....*the Keeper of the Heaven*
Al Haris Al Simak, Arabic...*the Keeper of the harmless wheat...*
Papsukal, Chaldean...*the Guardian-Messenger*
Sib- zi-anna, Euphraetean...*Shepherd of the heavenly flock*
Al Simak Al Ramih, Arabic....*the Unarmed,-The Healer*

Beta   3.6 golden yellow   on head of Arcturus

Nakkar, Nekkar, Arabic, Semitic....lit. *Pastoral powers,powerful -Shepherd's call*
Chaou, Yaou, or Teaou, Chinese...*to beckon, excite, or move...*

Gamma 3.1   on left shoulder

Seginus, from Ceginus, *Deliverer, Liberator*
Prona lycaona, Manlius- Latin....*(sloping —towards the 'greater bier') (Ash, the great assembly)*
Huen Ko, Chinese.....*the heavenly spear, (staff)*

Delta 3.5 pale yellow   20 degrees
        northeast of Arcturus.

No name...
Part of Tseih Kung, Chinese....*the seven princes.*

Epsilon   3 & 6 binary pale orange and bluish
        green (on) the belt of the Shepherd.

Al Mintaka Al Awwa, Arabic ...lit. *the preserved—(of) the Strong Shepherd*
Tso She Ti, Chinese.....*an officer, on the left hand of the emperor*

On waistcloth….later
Mirac, Mirak, trad. …*Loincloth*, lit…*having miraculous power*

Eta 2,   8 pale yellow   west of Arcturus on left leg

Al Mufrid Al Ramih, Arabic…lit. *the Liberator, the Resurrector*
Yew She Ti, Chinese…*the officer standing on the right hand of the emperor.*

Theta 4.1,   Iota triple 4.4, 4.5, 8,   and
Kappa double 4.5 and 6.6

Tseen Tsang, Chinese. *the heavenly lance (rod)*
Asellus, (Bayer)…*Powerful Word (authority)*

Mu ternary   4.2, 8, 8.5 flushed white, and
2-greenish white at head of spear or rod

Al Katurops, Arabic… *(on) herdsman's staff*
Clava, Latin…*staff or crook*

h or fl 38 5.5(on) reaping hook

Merga, Mergar, unknown…lit. *the conviction*

The ministry and leading and call
of the Great Shepherd…

Kentaurus—Decan of Bethulah

Beze, Hebrew…*despised*
Al Beze, Arabic…*the despised*

Rex Centaurus, Latin.....*King who comes smitten*
Al Kentaurus, later Arabic...*the One with many wounds*
Pholos Greek....*'one who died in consequence of exercising his virtue...'*
Chiron, Greek....*'one who renounced his mortality on earth in favor of Prometheus, (God's Promise) and was raised to the sky by *Jove'*
*(same as Jehovah).
Asmeath, Hebrew....*the sin offering*

Alpha Binary .2, 1.5 white and
yellowish on foot of centaur

Wazn, Arabic....*weight, loaded down, heavy, (with the guilt of the flock)*
Toliman, Uleg Beigh (Tartar astronomer, middle ages)....*heretofore, and hereafter*

Beta 1.2   near the right foreleg (west of Alpha)

Hadar, Semitic...*ground, earth, (honored, magnified)*
Agena, Burritt's map....*an intercession*
Mah Fuh, Chinese...*coming to die*

Gamma   2.4, and Tau 4.4 on right forefoot, (rear foot)

Koo Low, Chinese...*an arsenal tower*

Delta 2.8 on the tail

Ma Wei, Chinese....*on the tail, train, following*

Theta double and variable 2.2, 2.7,
14.3 red and bluish on shoulder

Menket, unknown origin...*ministry, and prayers completed*

33

Kappa

Ke Kwan, Chinese....*a cavalry officer*

Mu, Nu, Phi around the midsection towards shoulder

Wei, Chinese...*the balance*

I, g, k, and psi, with A

Choo, Chinese...*a pillar*
Connected to Victima, (mod. 'Lupus'), centaur's shield
was the place of Al Shamarili, and Kadb Al Karm, old
Arabic for *The palm branches, and the vine Branch.*

The King Jesus enters Jerusalem
The King with many wounds carries
the weight of the earth

Mozanaim, Hebrew/ Libra, Latin

Mozanaim; Moznayim, Hebrew... *a scale-beam*
'T', Hebrew, the letter Tau ...*symbolic of completion, a*
finishing
Al Zubena, Arabic...*the purchase*
Zuben, Syriac...*purchase*
Mazatho, Syriac....*scales*
Tarazu; Tarazuk, Persian....*shown as a figure lifting a*
scale in one hand, holding a lamb in the other.
Tolam; Tula, Sanscrit...*a balance lifting upwards*
Lambadia, Coptic...*station of propitiation* (gk)
Libra, Latin....*weighing*....bilancia, Italian...balance,
French
Waege, Angles...*wages, price*

34

Tien Ching, China...*a celestial balance*
Mizan, Arabic...*poured out for others*
Aliemin, Arabic...*the ransom*
Zugos, Greek...lit. *an attempt to devour (must be for where the claws are in place of the scales) as when Jesus surrendered in the garden of Gethsemene*

> A lpha1 and Alpha 2 on lower scale sun's ecliptic
> line widely double 3, 6 —pale yellow, light grey

Al Wazn Al Janubiyyah, Arabic...*the southern weight, the weight of the deficient, of the debtors*
Al Zuban Al Janubiyyah, or Zuben al Genubi, Arabic... *(the purchasing of the debtors, or deficient) purchasing of the deficient.*

> Beta   2.7 pale emerald on upper scale

Al Wazn Eschamali, *the weight lifting up, lifted*
Zuben El Chamali, or Al Zuben Al Shamaliyyah, Arabic.... *the purchase that covers, lifts up.*

> Gamma* reaching south towards Victima

Zuben Akrabi, Arabic....*price of the conflict*

> Delta 5 to 6.2 white   just east of beta

Sara Fasariva, Khorasmian...*one next to the Leader*
Fasariva, Sogdian

> Kappa, Lambda 5th magnitude
> on the sun's ecliptic line

Jih, China...*the sun*

   * In the scales when one scale descended with weight, it made the northern scale comparatively lighter and elevated it. Also notice that the Chinese called a star 'the sun' and it is on our sun's ecliptic line, as there was a solar eclipse for 3 hours during the crucifixion. Mt. 27:45
   And that the title seems to fit -Zaban (to push for A and B) as it seems one is pushing, lifting the other.

Other names associated with Mozanaim...

Al Gubi, Arabic....*the heaped up*

This is the cost / ransom -the expiation

Adom—Decan of Mozanaim

Adom, Hebrew...*the cutting off*
Sula, India...*the beam of crucifixion*
Arbedi, Persia...*a covering*
Sera, Coptic ...*triumph through great conflict*
Shih Tsze Kea, China...*A cross*
Southern cross, mod. English....*cross*

Alpha - triple 1, 2, and 6 on the foot

Crux, Tuscan.... lit. *Liberating King crucified (Nailed to tree, framework)*

Beta - on right hand

Mimosa, Noetic... lit. *strong wound seen, water pours out*

Gamma Crux1.8 to 2.4 the top or head

Delta Crux -on left hand

'...last seen on the horizon of Jerusalem (31 degrees N... by 46, 45 lat.) 33 AD.

This represents the crucifixion

Sura—Decan of Mozanaim

Sura, Semitic-Noetic....*Lamb,* Ulugh Beigh, says was anc. *a lamb*
Aseda, Hebrew...*to be slain*
Asedaton, Arabic...*the Sacrifice*
Hostia, Hyginus...*the Victim*
Victima Centauri, or
Victima, Latin...*the Victim*

Erroneously called 'lupus'

Few names remain for the individual stars of this constellation, however the Chinese have 2 names...

Alpha 2.6 on heel of figure

Yang Mun, or Men, Chinese...*the south gate*

Beta 3, 3.5 yellow -on feet of figure, (near spear tip of Centaurus)

Ke Kwan, Chinese...*a cavalry officer*

The stars in between Centaurus and Victima (where the shield is drawn) are described in various ways. The Arabians had them as Al Shamarili...the palm branches, and Kadb Al Karm ...The vine Branch.

Also a sense of libation or offering was represented here.

A letter known as Pilates report, said to be written by Pontus Pilate from the Archko volume transcribed from volumes in the Vatican library; (records from the Roman empire) and anc. Hebrew resources from centuries old volumes in Constantinople in the 1800's,...... (not recorded in the Gospels)

Pontus Pilate in this letter to the Roman senate describes a requested meeting with Jesus in his Praetorium....Pilate, describes both fear and admiration of Jesus in His presence, nonetheless requesting the Lord .... 'moderate'....his discourses, the Lord addresses Pilate in his 3rd response to him...

'...*Prince of the earth*'................. '*It is not in your power to arrest the Victim at the foot of the tabernacle of *expiation*' ....at which time the Lord exits through a curtain... 'like a bright shadow'.

Christ addressed Himself as *the Victim* to Latin Pilate, making it possible Pilate would make the connection that this was *Victima* in the ancient sky maps of the Latins and Etruscans.

Expiation- To atone for, make amends for, reparations.

This represents the lamb who was
slain, who was crucified

Ataroth—Decan of Mozanaim

Ataroth, Atarah, Hebrew...*the crown, (kingly)*
Al Iklil Al Shamaliyyah, Arabic... *the crown (ornament)*
of the north

Al Fakkah, Arabic...*the broken ring-dish*
Stephanos, Greek...*crown*
Corona Borealis, Latin...*the northern crown*
Kasah Shekesteh, Persian...*the broken platter*
Kas at al Salik, Arabic...*the broken Way, or path*

Alpha 2.4 brilliant white

Al Nair Al Fakkah, Arabic...*the Bright One of the dish*
Margarita Coronae, mod.... *the Pearl of the crown*
Gemma, Gemma Corona, mod.
Unopened buds in a coronal wreath... (hidden royalty)

Beta 4.

Nusakan, noetic, Semitic....lit. *privately broken -strength unseen, not shown...*

The theme is the crucifixion; He wore thorns as a crown in man's stead, as it was said at man's fall, 'cursed is the ground because of you....' '...thorns and thistles shall it bring forth to thee....' Gen 3: 17, 18.

Also He was accused of 'making Himself King', and thereby Pilate inquired of Him if He was a king. Jesus replied.....*'My kingdom is not of this world, else would my servants fight...... but now (at this time) is my kingdom not from here.'*

On his cross a sign written in 3 languages...*'This is Jesus the King of the Jews'. Mt. 27:37*

A King broken...died with a man's crown, thorns; a royal crown was His. The cross to purchase a kingdom His followers could enter.

The Northern Crown is beautiful, but incomplete or broken. This fits our condition, as the Paupers bowl, or broken platter, otherwise a beautiful creation, nonetheless we are broken, and he was broken on our behalf.

This fit's the theme of Libra. One pushing south, a royal King taking our penalty, moves (lifts) the other, fallen men, north.

This sign is vertical over Jerusalem once in every rotation of the earth.

Kingdom broken, King crucified

Akrabh, Hebrew/Scorpius, Latin

Akrabh, Hebrew...*a scorpion-conflict*
Al Akrab, Arabic...*the scorpion*
Akreva, Syrian...*scorpion*
Scorpios, Gk....*Great beast, Gk.....walking backwards,* Manlius
Scorpius, Latin....*scorpion*
Isidis, Coptic...*attack of the enemy*
Ghezhdum, Kazhdum, Persian...*a scorpion*
Girtab, Akkadian...*the siezer, stinger*
Vrouchicam, Indian... *wounding*
Koirughi, Turkish...*tailed*
Tien He, Chinese...*celestial scorpion*
Throwend, Anglo-Saxon...

Alpha -binary .7, 7 fiery red and emerald green in center of figure

Kalb al Akkrab, Arabic...*the heart of the scorpion (conflict)*
Kharthian, Coptic...*the heart*
Dharind, Khorasmian...*the seizer* Antares, Ant-ares Gk.... *rival of, or against Ares, (the ram) (rulership, reign) rebel.*

Beta- triple 2, 10, 4 pale white, —,
and lilac-on north side of head

Iklil Al Jabhah, Arabic, part of mansil (group asterism)...
crown of the forehead
Tien Sze, Chinese...*four horse chariot of heaven*
Graffias, unknown...*confronting to destroy*

Gamma-3.25 red on tip of southern claw

Zuban Al Akrab, Arabic...*the claws of the scorpion*
Al Zuban Al Janubiyyah, Arabic...*the claw of the south*
Chin Chay, Chinese...*the camp carraige*

Delta- 2.5 on forehead of creature

Al Jabhah, Arabic...*the forehead*
Dschubba, unknown...*striken for others*
Gis-gan-gu-sur, with beta and pi, Euphratean....*light of the hero in the midst of the abyss*

Theta   2.o red, on mid section of tail

Sargas, Ephratean, Noetic ...*where crushing strike begins...*
Located at point of tail where it curves, flicks, swings, upward

Lambda 1.7 at tip of tail

Al Shaulah, or Shaula, Arabic....*the sting*
Minamref, Coptic...*the sting*
Sarur, Euphratean...*stings strength fixed (to King)*

Upsilon 2.8 next to L at tail tip

Al Las 'ah, Arabic...lit. *the known strength of death (strongly crushed, sealed)*
Lesath, Noetic...*known life crushed completely separated*
Kow Kin, Chinese...L and U... *hook and latch, or locked*

The capture, sentencing, dying, and burial of the King... in the heart of the earth

Serpens—Decan of Akrabh

Alyah, Hebrew... *accursed's strength*
Al Rauda, old Arabic...*the pasture, enclosed sheep**
Al Hayyah, Arabic...*the snake*
Serpens, Latin...*the serpent*

Alpha - 3 pale yellow-orange

Unk Al Hayyah, Arabic... *neck of the snake (encompassing)*
Unuk, unknown...*neck*

Beta- double 3, 9.2 pale blue

Celbalrai... *hounding the shepherd (enfolding)*
Cheleb, unknown...*hounding, pursuing*

Theta -binary 4, 4.5 pale yellow and
golden yellow... (near end of tail)

Alya, Hebrew..., *limited, end*

Xi- 3.7 on lower part of body

Nan Hae, Chinese...*the southern sea*

This serpent is shown reaching for the Northern Crown previously described.

*The Arabic Al Rauda (enclosed sheep pasture) seems out of place for this constellation, however Abrahams' bosom was a real place described by Jesus. It was within sight of the abyss, where the divide was between those in Hades, and those in Paradise-(Abrahams's bosom) whereas both were in the earth....

Represents the same serpent, subtle, lying, deceiving, etc which deceived Eve in the Garden of Eden.

Afeichus—Decan of Akrabh

Afeichus, Hebrew....*serpent held*
Ophiuchus, Gk...*serpent holder*
Affalius, Persian...*serpent holder*
Serpentarius, Latin....*serpent treader*
Triophas, Hebrew...*treading underfoot*
Esculapius, Gk...*toiler*

Alpha 2.2 sapphire, on head

Al Rai, early Arabic...*the Shepherd -Lord's strength / reach extended*
Ras Al Hague, Arabic...*head of the Holder*
How, China...*the Duke*

Beta 3.3 yellow on east, right shoulder

Kalb Al Rai, Arabic...*the 'hounding' pursuing by the Shepherd*

Celbalrai, Noetic, Semitic....*hounded, pursued by the Shepherd*
Cheleb, Noetic, Semitic...*pursuer*

Gamma 4.3 below beta on right shoulder

Muliphen, unknown...*liberation begins*

Delta 2.8 deep yellow on right, eastern
wrist hand (viewed left side)

Yed, (prior), Noetic, Semitic....*hand*
Yad, Arabic...*hand*
Jed, Semitic....*hand*

Epsilon 3.8 red on left, western wrist
hand (viewed right side)

Yed (posterior,), Noetic, Semitic...*hand*

Eta 2.6 pale yellow on eastern knee (left)

Sabik, Noetic, Semitic....*Preceding One*
Saik, Noetic, Semitic....*the Driver*

Theta on eastern foot

Saiph, Noetic-Semitic....*bruised in the foot*

Lambda binary 4, 6 yellowish white, and smalt blue
Marfik, unknown....*elbow*

Rho on western foot above A Scorpio

Triophas, Hebrew....*treading under foot*
Carnebus, Noetic, Semitic...*the wounding, treading upon*

Other names associated with this sign,
Megeros....*contending*
Afeichus sometimes listed as the primary sign and not a decan

The great conflict unseen on earth,
tables beginning to turn

Marsic—Decan of Akrabh

Marsic, Hebrew....*the wounding*
El Giscale, Arabic....*the strong*
Engonasin, Greek...*who kneels*
Herakles, Gk...*Bruised Bruiser*
Hercules, Latin... *Deliverer—based on knowing (learning)*
the sacrifice
Genuflexus, Latin...*the kneeling One*
Clavator, Latin... *the club bearer*

Alpha -double both irregularly variable- 3.1, 3.9,5 to 7
Orange-red, bluish-green...on head

Ras Al Gethi, Arabic...*head of the Bruiser/Guardian-Warrior*

Beta 2.8 pale yellow on east shoulder

Korneforus, Greek...*kneeling Branch*

Lambda 4.8 deep yellow on east arm

Masym, or Ma'Asym, Hebrew... *the sin offering*

Xi double 4.8, 7 deep yellow on raised elbow

Marsic, Noetic-Semitic...*the wounding*

Omega 4.0 double on club

Caiam, Hebrew...*Punishing*

This figure is drawn with a foot on the head of the dragon
The Victor in the unseen conflict

Kesheth, Hebrew/ Sagittarius, Latin

Ashadha, Hindu... *Unconquered*
Pa Xut, Mesopotamian...*Dayspring*
Pi-maere, Coptic....*the going forth*
Croton, Greek...*Purchaser*
Sagittarius, Latin...*the Archer*
Kesheth, Hebrew...*the bow*
Keshth, Arabic...*the bow*
Kesith, Syriac...*the bow*
Belokpator, Gk...*Drawer of the arrow*
Toxotes, Greek...*the archer*
Danus, Sanscrit...*bow and arrow-armor*

Cuneiform inscriptions ...*'Illuminator of the great city'*....
Sayce transcribed from an inscription on a planisphere
'Utucagaba',... *'the light of the white face'*... Pinches
names as
'Udgudua'...*'the flowing day'*

Alpha - 4.0 *lower right knee*

Rukbat Al Rami, Arabic...— lit. *Resurrection's strong sign*
-the Lord's Power flows forth. (Raised.) or Glory of the
Resurrection

46

Beta - double 3.8 and 8, B2 4.4 *right heel*

Al Urkab, Arabic... *the reunion...lit. the Revived.*
Arkab, Semitic...lit. *Powerful Lord retains body*

Gamma —3.1 yellow on junction
point of arrow, hand and bow

Nash, Hebrew...lit. *Power to conquer death*
Al Nasl, Arabic...lit. *victory revealed*
Al Wasl, Arabic...lit. *vctory held*

Delta —double 3 & 14.5 Orange-yellow
&bluish...mid bow on forearm

Kaus Media, Arabic-Latin... Bow-middle lit. *holding power connected to crucifixion...middle*

Epsilon double 2 & 14.3 orange & bluish ....southern part of bow

Kaus Australis, Arabic-Greek...Bow-south lit. *holding power connected to the (crucifixion)...south*

Zeta-binary 3, 9 &4.4 .....arm body junction

Axilla, unknown...lit. *powerfully reaching support learned, known power*

Lambda 3.1 yellow northern part of bow

Kaus Borealis...Arabic, Greek... northern bow. lit. *holding power connected to the crucifixion ... north*

Sigma 2.3 on the vane of the arrow (feathers)

Nunki, unknown... lit. *hidden reunion with palm extended*

Pi — on right drawn shoulder

Al Baldah, Arabic...*the body learns of future power*

Other names associated with this sign not yet located

Naim, Hebrew...*Revived*
Nushata, Hebrew...*the victory draws numbers*
Terebellum, Latin...*staying to pray till power comes*
Al Naim, Arabic...*the Revived-resurrected multitude*
Al Shaula, Arabic...*the revelation of victory*
Al Warida, Arabic...*the victorious reunion*

The milky way seems to flow from this sign in the sky, even as 'a great cloud of witnesses'. The arrow is pointed at the tail of the scorpion.

The Resurrection and reunion

Lyra—Decan of Kesheth

Lyra, Latin...*harp/celebration ...lit. ...knowledge extends of the Lord's power*
Lira, Italian—*the harp/ celebration...lit. ...same as above*
Al Nasr Al Waki, Arabic...*the stone eagle of the desert... lit. Victorious Prince*
Al Nasr Al Tair, Arabic...*the flying eagle ...lit...all powerful Prince*

48

Alpha .3 pale sapphire on left base frame

Waki, Arabic...*lit.* ...*doubly connected to power extending, expanding*
Vega, Wega...*harp star, celebrating, rejoicing*
Tir-Anna, Akkadian... *Life of Heaven* — (Akkadians used this as their pole star.)
Dayan, Assyrian... *Judge of heaven*
Abhijit, Indian... *Victorious*

Beta variable & binary 3.4, 4.5 very white

Al Shilyak, Arabic...*the fishing eagle*
Shelyuk, same as above...*sent forth*

Gamma 3.3 bright yellow

Sulaphat, unknown.....*springing up*

Eta 4.4

Aladafar, unknown....*setting free*
Leen Taou, China...*'paths within the palace grounds'*

Mu 5.0 on the talons

Al Athfar, Arabic... *guarding the victory*

Victory. Heaven and earth rejoicing. He rejoices heaven

Ara—Decan of Kesheth

Mara, Hebrew...*destruction*
Al Mugamra, Arabic...*a finishing, completing*

Ara, Latin- Altare, It...*Altar*
Thusiasterion, Greek...*altar*
Al Mijmara, Arabic... *a censor*
Batillus, Latin...*an incense pan*

Alpha 2.9

Choo, Chinese...*a club or staff*

Beta 2, Gamma 2.8, Iota 9

Low, Chinese.... *trailing*

Delta and Zeta

...mark flame spilling to the south

> *This represents the sacrifice complete, and the sacrificial altar no longer necessary....even as the veil in the temple was torn. Also connected with punishing fire, spilling southward.*

Thuban—Decan of Kesheth

Thuban, Hebrew...*subtle, separated*
Al Dib, Arabic...*the reptile*
Drakon, Greek...*the dragon*
Draco, Latin...*the dragon*
Azhdeha, Persian...*man eating serpent*

Alpha 3.6 pale yellow

Thuban, Heb...*separated*
Al Tinnin, Arabic... *devouring serpent*

Al Dhibah, Arabic...*the hyenas*
Al Waid, Arabic...*to be destroyed*

Beta binary 3 & 14 yellow on head, or eyes of creature

Rastaban, Heb...*head of the separated*
Al Ras Al Thuban, Arabic...*the head of the separated*

Gamma double 2.4 & 13.2 orange

Al Ras al Tinnin, Arabic...*head of the serpent*
Eltanin, short for above...*the serpent*

Delta 3.1 deep yellow

Al Tais, Arabic...*the goat*
El Asieh, Heb, Noetic... *the bowed down*

Zeta 3.0

Al Dibah, Arabic...*the hyena,*
Al Dhi Bain...*lying in wait (for camel's foal)*

Iota 3.6 orange

Al Dhili...*the male hyena*
El Athik...*the fraudful*

Lambda 4.1 orange

Giansar, unknown...*punished enemy*

Mu binary 5, 5.1 brilliant & pale white

Al Rakis, Arabic...*the dragon mouth*

Xi 3.8 yellow on dragon's tongue

Grumium, unknown...*the subtle*

Not much need to clarify what this sign represents....but that it is being cast down...as Jesus saw the devil as lightning cast down, in a falling position.

Gedi, Hebrew/ Capricorn, Latin

Gedi, Hebrew...*cut-off, hewn down*
Al Gedi, Arabic...*the cut-off, hewn down*
Gedi, Syrian...*cut off*
Capricornus, Latin...*atonement sinking down*
Semi capran-fish, Latin...*goat-fish*
Altera solis porta, Latin...*the southern gate of the sun.*
Hupenius, Coptic...*station of bearing*
Bushgali, Bahi, Vahik, Goi, Persian...*goat*
Gadjo, Syrian ...*goat*
Nahi, Pahlavi...*goat*
Ughlak, Turk...*goat*
Aigokereus, Greek...*the goat*
Mo-Ki, Chinese...*goat-fish*

Alpha double 3.2, 4.2 yellow and triple, 3, 11.5, 11.5 pale yellow, ash and lilac — on horn

Al Gedi, Arabic... *the slain*
Prima and segunda Giedi, Latin...*the slain*

Beta 1, and 2 -2.5, 6 yellow and sky blue —on forehead

Al Sa'd Al Dhabih, Arabic...*the Fortunate one (Chosen) of the slaughterers*

Gamma 3.8 on tail

Al Sa'd Al Nashirah, Arabic...*the Fortunate, the Bringer of Good Tidings*

Delta 3.1 on tail east of gamma

Al Dhanab Al Jady, Arabic.....later Deneb Algedi...*tail, train of the slain, hewn down...* (with gamma were Al Muhibban)...*the two friends*

Lambda 5.4 on end of tail

(with other nearby stars) were Tien Luy Ching, Chinese... *the heavenly walled castle*

Mu 5.24 end of tail

Kuh, Chinese...*weeping*

Nu 4.7 on lower neck

Al Shat, Arabic....'*the Sheep that was to be slaughtered by the adjacent stars Beta...Dhabih*

Phi 4.3

Yue, Chinese....*battle axe*

The goat of atonement as shown in Leviticus. One who carried away our sins, but returned alive again leading to the waters. Scapegoat for mankind.

Scham—Decan of Gedi

Sagitta, Latin...*arrow*
Scham, Heb..... *destroying, desolating*
Al Sahm, Arabic....*arrow*
Telum, Latin....*dart, weapon*
Saetta, Italian....*arrow*
Pfeil, German...*arrow*
Fleche, French....arrow
Otysys Kalem, Turkish...*smooth arrow*
Hes, or Hets, Hebrew....*arrow*
Tigris, Armenian-Persian...*smooth arrow*

Alpha...

Sham, Arabic....*arrow*

Beta

Kaus, Semitic trad. ...*bow*

None of the stars of this constellation were universally named, however sometimes Alpha is named 'Sham' same as meaning in Arabic, and Italian, and Beta on the shaft has been named 'Kaus' (bow). An arrow (word) flying through the sky with the bow (power to send) with it.

This is a description of the gospel, in which Jesus preached and was the main character involved, preaching that He himself would be crucified.....and rise again the 3rd day....at the heart of the gospel. The bow or Kaus on the shaft represents the power of the news to go forth.... or equipped with power/ included.

As Paul stated in Romans '....I am not ashamed of the gospel of Christ: for it is the power of God unto salvation to everyone that believes; to the Jew first, and also to the Greek. ' Romans 1: 16

This is the arrow of the Judge, specifically the prophetic statements regarding the crucifixion, and thereafter the resurrection, which Jesus prophesied would be fulfilled in Himself

Neshr—Decan of Gedi

Neshr, Hebrew...*an eagle*
Aquilla, Latin... *the eagle*
Alub, Gherges and Shahin Tara zed, Persian....*the star striking falcon*
Al Okab, Arabic.... *the black eagle*
Adler, German...*eagle*
*Aquilla Promethei, Latin... *God's promised; fishing eagle swooping down*
*Jovis Armiger, Latin...'*armor-bearing bird of Jove*'...
Taushaugjil, Turkish...*hunting eagle*

*Both the names Promethei (God's promised one, Greek equivalent of Hebrew Mashiach, Messiah), and Jove, Jovis (corruption of an early form of Jehovah), were gentile, (Latin, Greek, etc...) names slightly altered over time of the original names or titles of the original God and Savior. The eagle is represented in Ezekiels' vision Ch. 1, and Johns' in Revelation Ch. 4.

Alpha 1.3 pale yellow

Al Tair, Arabic...*the eagle, wounding*
Al Nasr Al Tair, Arabic...*the Princely eagle*
Erigu, anc. Mesopotamia...*the powerful bird*

Sadmasij, Korasmian...*the noble falcon*
Shad Mashir, Sogdian...*the noble falcon*

Beta 3.9 pale orange

Shahin, Persian...*falcon*
Al Shain, Semitic....*bright, scarlet*

Gamma 3 pale orange

Tara zed, Persian....*stricken (star), wounded*

Delta

Al Cair, Arabic...*the piercing*

Epsilon 4.3 and Zeta 3.3 green

Al Dhanab Al Okab, Arabic...*the tail of the eagle, wounded
in the heel*
Deneb...*tail*

The very arrow of the previous constellation sent out
with power is the same word that wounds the eagle,
seemingly intercepting it, as it descends toward the
seas. As stated before seas represent humanity.

*This reviews the events and time as Christ
reveals in scripture he was to die, and thereafter
take up his life again. His ascension.*

Dalaph—Decan of Gedi

Dalaph, Hebrew...*pouring out of water*
Ieroz Icthuz, Greek...*sacred fish...* (Christians identify
with the fish symbol)
Delphinus, Latin...*Dolphin...similar to Hebrew name, yet
the animal is shown, leaping out into the air in joy*
Shi Shu Mara, later Zizumara, Hindu...*a porpoise*

Alpha, 4.0 pale yellow; Beta, binary,
4.0 and 6.0 greenish and dusky;
With Gamma, Double 4.0 and 5.0; and Delta.

Al Ukud, Arabic...*pearls or precious stones adorning Al
Salib*
lit. *(Crucifixion) or 'nailed hands' connected to Liberty*
Al Salib....lit. *powerful exortations*

Epsilon 4.0

Al Amud al Salib, Arabic...trad. *pillar of the cross*
lit. *-teaching of the baptism to come*
Al Dhanab al Dulfim, Arabic...*the dolphin's tail*
Hindu's (asterism)-'Cravishtha' ...*most favorable*
Dhanishtha, -*richest*....and 'the Vasus'-*bright or good
ones*

*This constellation as it literally appears on a clear night
to be a water jar tilted in the position of pouring out, or
about to pour out...*the figure usually drawn as a dolphin
or fish, appears to be the top of a tilted water urn.

Arabian astronomers adopted the Greek name
Dulf im, which one of their chroniclers described as

57

"...A marine animal friendly to man, attendant upon ships to save the drowning sailors"

So the fish, dolphin fits the idea, but is incomplete without the Hebrew base definition of the outpouring of water.

Persian map shows both stream of water and a fish; however the Hebrew name, and the 2 star names give a clear definition of the main idea.

The idea of a Dolphin, and the name for pouring out of water Heb. Dalaph, being so similar looks like an error in translation (Latin-Delphinus).

However it is not the case. If you follow the path of languages from Latin, to Etruscan, to Lydian (Lud, son of Shem), to Shem. Therefore the Latin alphabet is also a Semitic, or Noetic one, as the Semitic itself was from the original language spoken by Noah.

All versions of Alpha-bet are descended from the same translations of the individual letters, just slightly varied in arrangement.

'Julius Schiller knew some of its stars as the water pots of Cana.' * Star Names their Lore and Meaning...Richard Hinckley Allen

This also bears out the meaning as Jesus by His being stricken, we were given the waters of life.

The Greek and Latin definitions may have come from the original Hebrew name, and the dolphin leaping out of the water, relates the joy of the out pouring.....and this leads us into our next constellation...

This seems to represent the ascencion and promise of the living waters to come.

Deli, Hebrew/Aquarius, Latin

Al Sakib Al Ma, Arabic...*the Pourer of water*
Delu, Arabic...*water urn*
Deli, Hebrew...*water urn*
Daulo, Syrian...*the water jar*
Dol, or Dul, Persian...*water jar*
Hupei Tirion, Coptic...*station of pouring out*
Hydrokoeus, Greek...*Pourer forth of water*
Aquarius, Latin....*Water Pourer*
Waeter-gyt, Anglo-Saxon...*the Water Pourer*
Pao Pigh, mod Chinese...*precious vase*

To the Han dynasty it was the symbol of the emperor Tchoun Hin in whose reign was a great deluge......sounds like biblical Noah. However erroneous the assignment to Noah was....it reveals that the signs were known in Noah's days.

Alpha 3, 2 pale yellow

Al Sa'd Al Melik, Arabic...*Fortune (blessing) of the King*
Al Sa'd Al Mulk, Arabic...*Fortune (blessing) of the Kingdom*
Sadalmelik... Same meaning from the above names
El Melik, Semitic...*the King*

Beta 3.1 pale yellow

Al Sa'd Al Su'ud, Arabic...*Blessing of the blessed*

Gamma 4.1 greenish

Sa'd Ali Biyah, Arabic...*Blessing of the secret (hidden) places*

Delta 3.4 on right leg

Al Shi' at, Arabic...*the wish, Hope*
Sheat, variation of above

Associated with Hasisadra, or Xasisadra, the 10th antediluvian king and hero of the deluge in the old Euphratean cultures. This would be Noah, who was tenth from Adam. But the Water-pourer does not represent Noah in a literal sense, but symbolically. It has a meaning that would be revealed more than 2000 years later. But for the sake of understanding the post flood mindset....Noah lived near where the headwaters of the Araxes, the Tigris, and the Euphrates rivers begin. The first towns of the area were on the Araxes, or Araks (river of the ark) in Armenian Terapheminim, (region of the eight; 'terra-firma') which flowed from Ararat ....where Noah was...and the cultures of Mesopotamia, situated on near the Euphrates, and Tigris -one could see how this association was formed, but as stated this sign has a Spiritual meaning.

Epsilon 3.4

Al Sa'd Al Bula, Arabic...*Blessing of those who drink in*
Al Bali, Arabic...*Churches strength increases*

Theta 4.3 on belt or waist

Ancha, unknown...*vessel of pouring out*

Xi 5.5 at opening of water vase

Situla, Latin...*water jar...from sitis, thirst.* Therefore, *Thirst quencher* ... would fit.
Al Dalw, Arabic....and
Satl, Arabic...similar definitions as above

Lambda 3.8 red

Udor, or Vdor, Greek, *the Outpouring, the water*

Omicron 4.7

Al Sa'd Al Mulk, Arabic...*Blessing of the Kingdom*

Pi 4.8

Seat, as named by Grotius...

Other names
Mon, Egyptian...lit. *Outpouring seen multiplying*

This is the outpouring of the Holy Spirit on Pentecost.

Al Hut Al Janubiyy—Decan of Deli

Al Hut Al Janubiyy, Arabic...*the large fish of the south*
Pisces Australis, Latin....*southern fish*
Pesce Australe, Italian...*southern fish*
Sudliche fisch, German...*southern fish*
Southern fish, English

Alpha 1.3 reddish on the mouth of fish

Fum Al Hut, Arabic...*mouth of the fish, or*

Fomal Haut.....*mouth of the fish*

Beta 4, 3 and 8 double on belly or gills

Al Nair, Arabic...lit. *given unseen Power, (in-through belly)*

Gamma, on tail

Al Dhanab, Arabic...*the tail*

This is the church symbolized as a fish drinking in. The upper room in Acts 2.

Pekasus—Decan of Deli

Pekasus, Semitic...*Chiefs (Lord's) swift One*
Pegasus, Greek and Latin... *Chiefs swift One*
Alatus, (Alfonse Tables) *winged*
Pegasus Equus (Almagest 1551) *swiftly arriving horse*
Pegasus Equus Alatus (17th century astronomers) *same*

Associated with fountain springs, glad tidings, and swiftness...

Alpha 2.5 white on shoulder

Marchab, Semitic...*saddle, ship, vehicle...as to be carried, Carrier-lifter*
Markab, same as above...*a Help in carrying, lifting*
Matn al Faras, Arabic...loc. name..*the horses' shoulder—*

Beta 2.2-2.7 variable deep yellow on elbow of forearm

Sheat, Semitic...lit.*crushed body's (church) life powerfully guarded, uplifted*

Mankib Al Faras, Arabic....*the withers, under girding horse*
Menkib, Uleg Beigh...lit. *Waters of life given reaching house(body)*

Gamma 3 white on back of horse

Al Genib, Arabic...lit. *the Good news extended to house, (temple)*

Delta ...

This is the same as Alpha Andromedae, a shared or common star.

This, with alpha, beta and gamma Pegasus form a quadrangle called Al Dawl, Arabic... *the water bucket.* This huge square which outlines the body of the figure is a double asterism in the Indian nakshatras; Purva, former and Uttara, latter the Bhadrapada...*beautiful, auspicious, or happy feet...*
Also Proshtha-Pada translated *Footstool Feet..*

Epsilon triple 2.5, 11.5, 8 and 8
yellow, yellow, blue on mouth

Enif, unknown ...lit. *Life unseen unifies*
Al Anf, Arabic....lit. *The Unifier*
Fum, Arabic...*mouth*
Al Jah, Arabic...*the mouth*

Zeta 3.7 light yellow in neck

Homam, Noetic...*the Waters*
Al Hammam, Arabic...*the Whisperer*

Eta 3.2 double

Matar, Noetic...*the Overflow*
Al Sa'ad Al Matar, Arabic...*The Fortunate Rain*

Theta 3.8, 4.8

Biham, Noetic....*offspring, young*
Sa'ad Al Bahaim, Arabic... *Blessing of the thirsty*

Kappa 4.8, 5.3, 10.8 yellowish and orange

Jih, Chinese...*the sun*

Lambda 4.1 3.4 and or Mu

Sa'ad Al Bari, Arabic....*Fortune of the excelling one*
Sa'd Al Nazi, Kazwini...*Fortune of the (Prince) pasture seeker*

Tau 4.5

Sa'ad Al Na Amah, Arabic...*crossbars on a well*
Al Karab, Arabic...*the bucket rope*
Salma, or Salm, Noetic...*a leathern* bucket*

*Leathern makes a reference to the covering of Adam and Eve.

This is unmistakably the Day of Pentecost, Hebrew feast of first-fruits Shavuot. The Holy Spirit and His Living Waters flowing into and through the disciples beginning. It seems more and more apparent that the symbol of a horse throughout these signs, whether it be half drawn, as in Kentaurus, and Keshith, or partly drawn as in Pekasus symbolizes Spirit, and/or spiritual; so that those represented the Spirit-Man, who is Jesus...

the God-Man, and Pekasus represents the Spirit as an individual coming to the aid of man. God is a Spirit. And in the natural sense the Equiine are a carrier of men, and a strong help.

This seems to symbolize the Holy Spirit himself, Heaven's help to mankind coming down filling and guiding...

Azel—Decan of Deli

Cygnus, Latin...circling
Azel, Hebrew...*going and returning. lit. powerful word of life taught (gospel)*
Al Dajajah, Arabic...*the hen. .... lit. liberated leaders extend strength to separated, (those outside)....reaching out. The outreach*
Cygnus, Latin... *going and returning (circling)*
Cycnos, Greek...*circling swan*
Quasi Galli Rosa, Riccolli...*Gallic Cross*
Cigno, Italian...*the swan*
Cygne, French...*the swan*
Cisne, Spanish...*the swan*
Schwan, German...*the swan*
Gallina, unknown...lit. *Gospel going forth*
Olor...*swan*

Alpha 1.4 brilliant white on tail

Al Dhanab Al Dajajah, Arabic...loc. *the tail of the hen* lit *expanding body of the delivered...the Gospel goes forth*
Deneb, Semitic...loc. *the tail* lit. *the expanding body (church)*

Arided, Al Ridhadh, Arabic...El Rided.....lit. *(The) liberated from death*
Os rosae, Cassius...*the recently renewed, revived*

Beta-double binary 3, 5, and 7 topaz
yellow and sapphire blue on beak

Al Bireo, unknown origin...*the witness*
Al Minliar al Dajajah, Arabic... loc. *the hen's beak*...lit *the preaching of the Delivered (Gospel)*
Hierizim, Riccioli...*separated given life as word (gospel) flows forth*

Gamma 2.7 hen's lower breast area

Sadr, Semitic...*who returns as a circle*
Al Sadr al Dajajah, Arabic... ...lit. *the circling of the Delivered*
Tien Tsin, China...with a, b, and d *was the name of a city*

Epsilon 2.6 yellow hen's southern wing

Gienah, unknown...lit. *Word extending to separated (isolated). (preaching the Gospel)*
Al Janah, Arabic... *the wing*

Pi 4.8 on end of tail

Azelfafage, Hebrew-Semitic...trad. *shining forth*
Azelfage, Bayer...lit. *circling word of life.*

Omega 5.5 and 10 - 5 degrees northeast of Deneb

Al Rukbah al Dajajah, Arabic...loc. *the hen's knee*...lit. *the delivered (Gospel) of the Redeemer*

The Arabic name Dajajah seems to both represent the Gospel, (Good news) and Deliverance simultaneously. It is difficult to describe in a few words the depth and width of the meaning of this.

The Arabic titles for the names here, and in many other cases are physical descriptions giving us the location on the figure, but which itself expresses and characterizes something greater. In this one the Hebrew names and Latin, give us the specific expressions of the character of the figure. The circling, and the shining forth, etc.

This figure represents the gospel (good news) going forth after Pentecost, via the disciples, at Jerusalem, and going and returning carrying the story of the cross, (the Northern Cross). In Arabic it is described in the feminine (hen) even as the church is described in the feminine sense.

Dagim, Hebrew/Pisces, Latin

El Haut, anc. ....*the fish*
Dagim, or Dagaim, Hebrew...*the fish multiplied*
Al Haut, Al Hut, Arabic...*the fish*
Nuno, Syrian...*fish extended out*
Pi-Cot Orion, Coptic...*fish of him that comes*
Icthues, Gk...*fish*
Pisces, Latin...*fish multiplying*
Peisun, Anglo-Norman...*fish*
Mahik, Persian...*fish*
Balik, Turkish...*fish*
Al Samakah, or Al Samakatain, Arabic...*the fish, increased*
Fixas, Anglo Saxon...*extending support*
Shang Yu, Chinese...*the Lord expands*

Alpha double 4 @ 5.5 pale green @ blue

Ton-Pinon, Ptolemy-Gk. Probably a Coptic name....*knot of the fish. lit. sign of the multiplying—Word(s) extends to the fish (church) vision of multiplying*
Okda, Semitic...F. Rolleston...*the united*
Ukd al H' aitain, Arabic...*union in the place of the fish*
This asterism may represent Jerusalem, from which the (fish) proceed.

Beta 4.5 on fish's mouth

Fum al Samakah, Arabic (Al Achsasi)...*the fish's' mouth (the westernmost fish)**
Al Samaca, Arabic.....F. Rolleston...*the upheld*

Kappa, Lambda 4 and 11

Yun Yu, Chinese...*cloud and rain*

The fish are shown as 2 and the western fish swims rather freely toward the Waterpourer, while the northeastern fish swims but is hindered, into Andromeda's lap, overlapping parts of Andromeda, revealing further characteristics of the fish's progression.

This is the church (fish) multiplying and expanding outward.

Al Risha—Decan of Dagim

Al Risha, Arabic...*the cord, the band.*
U-OR, anc. Egypt...*to flow forth, path, Way*
Kuton, Coptic...*cord*

Commissura Piscium, Pliny...*the fish's (church's) commission*
Kaht, Persian...*cord (Lunar asterism)*
Al H' ait al Kattaniyy, Arabic...*the flaxen thread*
Vincla, Cicero...*the bonds*

Often considered part of the constellation
Pisces...Anciently a separate sign.

Delta 4.1 on cord of western fish about midpoint

Kuton, Coptic....*cord, or thread* lit. *holding true to the cross expands*
Al Risha, Arabic...*the cord*

Alpha Pisces through to the northern fish's' tail

Linum boreum, Hevelius...*northern thread or linen*

Epsilon Pisces through to the southern fish's tail

Linum austrinum, Hevelius...*southern thread or linen*

The theme here with the cord knotted, and limited in the *Linum Boreum*, rather taut, reveals the attempted limitations the world will put on believers, *to restrict their path, their work,.....* Whereas the *Linum Austrinum shows the cord not limited* as the westernmost of the fish swims toward the Waterpourer of the previous constellation.... see 'Gospel in the Stars' by Joseph Seiss.

*The cord here represents the path,
stream, Way, and life of the fish.*

Kifaus—Decan of Dagim

Kifaus, *Arabic.... *from a Semitic root meaning Ransom, or Reconcile...(er)*
Kepheus, Kefeus,* Aratos from Gk....*Consoler, Counselor*
Cepheus,* Latin...*King of the redeemed, or ransomed...*
Cefeo*, Italian....see above
Aner Basilhios, Nonnus-from Gk....*lit.-King of the congregation..... (Churches)*
Iasides, Caesar Germanicus...literal....*One who extends Power and authority.*
**Al Multahab, Arabic...from Inflammatus *or The One who is Lord over fire...the fires...signifying troubles-tribulation* (see Daniel in Babylon, spec. Shadrach, Meshach, and Abednego)
Hyk, Ethiopian...*King*
Phicares, Persian...*delivering Word to the most needy*

Kaph, Kaf, or Caph, all stand for the letter associated with 'K' Gk.-Kappa...*and it represents holding something or something held....*

*These names are derived anciently from the Hebrew-semitic origins-Kaphar....*means to console, Pardon, forgive, reconcile,*
Kopher .....*means to ransom, or a ransom*
Kippur....*means atonement (as in Yom Kippur)*

The title for this constellation therefore must be associated with One who atones, ransoms, with the corresponding inference of being royal, at the highest place in the heavens.
**Other names as 'fire' represents that He is King in the midst of the fires of tribulation, persecutions...

and reaches to console Andromeda, (pre-ordained, the church).

Alpha 2.5 white...right arm

Al Dera- imin, Arabic...lit. ...*The Liberator's Life like a river reaching His multiplied. (Extender of authority)*

Beta3.3, 8 white and blue

Al Firk, Arabic...lit. *The Holder of the Congregation*

Gamma 3.5 yellow -on left knee

Al Rai, Arabic...*The Shepherd*...lit. *The Lord's powerful reach*

Eta and Sigma 4.0 on right wrist

Al Kidr, Arabic...lit. *The Keeper of the delivered*

Kappa, 4.4,-8

Shang Wei, Chinese...*the Higher, Highest Guard*

Other names associated with Cepheus

Cheicus, caucus, Hebrew...*comes as in a circle*
Al Derab, or Al Deraf, Arabic....*coming in a circle*
Kurmah, Hebrew...lit. *having power to deliver*

This is the Lord exhorting and counseling his church, giving them authority.

Sirra—Decan of Dagim

Sirra, Hebrew...*the chained, lit., same*
Al Mara, Arabic...*the afflicted*
Andromeda, Gk... *ruler of men, Man-ruler*
Ksunos aster, Gk...lit. *church martyrs*
Virgo Devota, Ceasar Germanicus...*devoted virgin*

> Alpha double 2.2, and 11 white
> and purple-ish...on head

Al Ras al Mar'ah al Musalsalah, Arabic (Ptolemy's time)...
the head of the woman in chains.
Alpheratz, Alpherat, Semitic...*the broken down*
Sirrah, Semitic...*navel*

    * With a, b, and c Pegasus, this star formed the 'great square'...and in Hindu lunar astronomy constituted a double Nakshatra, 24th and 25th...the Purva, and Uttara Bhadrapadas...*'the former and latter beautiful and auspicious feet';* also given as Proshthapadas...*'Footstool feet'.*

    The early Arabic astronomers had this star Alpha Andromeda connected with Pegasus as even directly connected to it, as having been birthed from there.

> Beta 2.3 yellow on side

Mirach, Semitic...lit. *streams extent (way) (of the fish) begins (to be) strongly hunted, (pursued, trap) believers hounded....persecution*
Al Janb al Musalsalah, Arabic...*the side of the chained contented woman*
Al Kalb al Hut, Arabic...*the *hounding of the fish*

* Kalb in these themes from the Arabic seems to generally represent the hounding, or troubling -and not usually the animal (dog) specifically. The fish is transposed partly over the lap of the Chained woman, suggesting that they are different characteristics of the same body represented....as here it is the church. This reveals the progression of the fish to this point.

Gamma binary-perhaps ternary, 2.3, 5.5, and 6.5, orange, emerald, and blue on chained foot

Al Anak al Ard, Arabic, *said to be a small badger like animal*....lit. *The Fish withheld*
Al Rijl al Musalsalah, Arabic...*the woman's' foot*
Alamac, Alphonse tables....*lives delivered over*
Alamech, Flamsteed tables...lit. ...*the lives hunted, persecution*
Al Amak, Joseph Seiss...lit. ...*the imprisoned*
Al Maach, Arabic-Semitic F. Rolleston... *struck down*

The small predatory animal resembling a badger will come up again in another constellation, and reveals a creature that preys on venomous snakes and other malignant creatures.

Zeta 4.9 train of garment

Adhil, Semitic... *afflicted teachers*
Al Dhail, Arabic...*the imprisoned teach*

Psi binary 4.9, and 6.5 yellow and green, and X, 5

Keun Nan Mun, Chinese...*the camps' south gate*

Other names associated with Andromeda

Al Mosel Salah, Arabic...*delivered from Hades, Sheoel*
Misam Al Thuraiya, Arabic...*the assembled*

Other names cont'd

Andromedia, Gk...*future men ruler*
Desma, Semitic....*bound*
Mizar, Semitic....*the bound*

*This sign represents the church persecuted,
oppressed, hated, and restricted by / in the world.*

Taleh, Hebrew/Aries, Latin

Taleh, Hebrew... *Lamb*
Al Hamal, Arabic...*Sheep, gentle, merciful.*
Al Kabah Al Alif, Arabic...*the tame Ram.*
Amroo, Amru, Syrian... *Lamb*
Ammon, Anc. Egypt...*established reign*
Krios, Kriya, Gk...*Ram*
Aries, Latin...*Ram*
Pe Taugu, Chinese...*white sheep*
Ku, anc. Euphratean...*the Prince, or the Leading one, the
Ram that led the heavenly flock.*
Kuzi, Turk...lit. *Hold connected to word (gospel) extended*
Mesha, Sanskrit...*Freedom, Liberty*
Mesham, Tamil..." "　..............*flowing*

Alpha 2.3 yellow above head

El Nath Semitic...lit. *the multiplied's strong Protector..*
Al Natih, Arabic....Kwazini, Ulegh Beigh..." " *"protection
extended*

Al Ras Al Hamal, Arabic...*The Head of the sheep.*
Dil Kar, anc. Cuneiform inscription... *Proclaimer of the dawn.*
Dil-Gan, " " " .... *Messenger of Light*
Ayil, Hebrew...*Powerfully extends knowledge, increasing knowledge*
Ailuv, Assyrian...*Powerful teaching fixed to union*
Aloros, Akkadian.... anc. 'Associated with the first of the 10 'mythical' kings anterior to the flood.'

Adam through Noah makes 10 patriarchs. This is interesting but an error unless you consider that the Son of Man is the 2nd Adam.

Beta 2.9 pearly white western horn

Al Sharat, Arabic...*the sign*...lit. *the victory over death's power begins as strong sign*
Al Sharatain, Arabic...*the signs*

Gamma double 4.5, 5 bright white
and grey west of Beta on horn

Mesharetim, Hebrew...*ministers*...lit. *Way of Life conquering death a sign, church grows.*
Mesarthim, same...lit. *protected church increases*

Delta 4.6 on belly

Al Butain, Arabic...*the belly*...lit. *unified church (body) multiplied*
Botein, Semitic...lit. *praying church multiplied*

———————

The Shepherd, the Head, next—the signs, the ministers on horn, next - the unified, praying church multiplied, on belly. This is a prophetic layout for the order of the church, showing the Lord being the Head in charge, followed by signs of such expounded through ministers, and the praying, united church (body) multiplies. It still amazes me this was laid out in antediluvian times 3 thousand plus years before Christ was born.

The likes of Calvin, Martin Luther, John Huss, and many others numerous reflect a turning point in church history. -Whereas once the church was early on a minority in sovereign nations, and persecuted at times.... now the persecuted church shows forth the undeniable power of God, the saving power of the Messiah, revealed previously in Pisces as Cepheus...and now stands in to take her place in kingdoms to rule in righteousness, revealed in real historical time and best reflected by individuals such as Elizabeth 1 of England......

Simultaneously, the Church needed physical protection at times from wrong thinking religiously motivated persecutors...IE inquisitions, Jihad's, pogroms, outright invasions, ...which led some rulers to stand in defense of the church. Early examples of this would be England's Elizabeth 1, or Sweden's Gustav Adolphus in the 16th and 17th centuries.

Another aspect of this sign is in the title Kuzi which means expansion -holds linked to Gospel going forth. This in a historical sense can be said to be fulfilled around 1500 AD when God enlarged Japeth as Noah prophecied in Genesis; as the European nations expanded east and west bringing the story of the cross with them in one form or another.

The head of the church re-establishes it in authority, honor, and defensive might.

Cassiopeia—Decan of Taleh

Kaff Al Hadib, Arabic...*hand stained with henna...* lit. *having the Power to free the prisoners.*
Cassiopeia, Semitic... *enthroned, beautiful*
Jostandis, Lithuanian...*girded, girding*
Set, anc. Egyptian Hieroglyphs...*Set up*

Alpha multiple and slightly variable
2.2 to 2.8 pale rose on chest

Shedar, Semitic...*the Freed, Freedom*
lit...*Starting to free captives*
Zedaron, Semitic, lit. ...*Word of life liberates strongly, souls multiplied*
Al Dhat al Kursiyy, Uleh Beigh...*the freed from the judgments*
Seder, Semitic...*delivered from persecution, Life begins*

Beta 2.4 white on throne, or chair

Caph, Chaph, or Kaff, Semitic...*to possess, have, own*

Gamma 2 and 11 brilliant white on waist

Cih, Semitic...lit. ... *set free*

Delta 3.0 on knee

Al Ruch bah, Arabic...loc. ...*the knee.* lit. ...*The Lord committed to deliver prisoners / houses divided.*

Ruchbah, Semitic...*set apart*

Zeta, and Lambda 4 and 5 on face

Foo Loo, Chinese...*a by-path*

Theta 4.4, Mu triple 5.1, 10.5, and 11 deep yellow, blue, and ruddy on elbow of raised arm

Al Marfik, Arabic...loc. *the elbow* lit. *the blessing (ed) expands and holds*
Marfak, unknown...*Powerful blessing established*

This is the congregation liberated, extending, making itself ready. Freed from persecutions and imprisonments. Rededicating, re-vitalized.

Kaitos—Decan of Taleh

Belua, Almagest (Ptolemy), and Alphonse tables ...*the beast, or monster... a beast of the sea...see rev. 13.*
Kaitos, unknown... *destroying monster*
Al Ketus, Arabic, lit. ...*destroyer set for destruction*
Khetos, Aratos, Gk... *whale*
Cetus, Latin, since days of Vitruvius ...*whale*
Orphis, Orphos, Gk., lit. ...*knows it's end*

Alpha 2.9 bright orange on monster's jaws

Menkar, Hebrew-Semitic tr. ...*chained enemy*

Beta 2.4 yellow on the tail towards the south

Deneb Kaitos, Arabic...*tail of the beast or sea monster*

Al Dhanab al Kaitos al Janubiyy, Arabic....*beast moving towards the south*
Diphda, Semitic...tr. ...*overthrown, thrust down*

Gamma double 3.5 and 7 pale yellow and blue on face

Al Kaff al Jidhmah, Arabic...*the holder of many prisoners*

Delta 3.9 topaz yellow

Al Batn al Kaitos, Arabic...loc. *the whale's belly...* lit. *the dwelling of the persecuters*
Batenkaiton, Alphonse tables... same as above but adding *–resisting church increase*

Eta 3.6 yellow

Deneb, Dheneb, Semitic...*tail (trail)*

Iota 3.6 bright yellow

Deneb Kaitos Al Shamaliyy, Arabic...*tail (trail) of the beast in the north*

Omicron variable 1.7 to 9.5,
flushed yellow in the beast's neck

Mira, Semitic tr. ...*rebel*

Cetus is usually represented as laying hold with bear-like paws and claws on the river Eridanus which river will be described shortly...

The title translation 'whale' was surely a simplification for a complicated figure, but an incomplete title. It has some whale like features, particularly the narwhale, which contains a tusk-like horn protruding from its

79

head. In this figure it is lunging at the underbelly of Taurus, with this tusk, or horn.

The combinations of the creature can best be described simply as a beast coming out of the sea, is internally changeable, a provocateur (the horn), and laying hold of destruction.

Some other names for this figure,

Al Nitham, Arabic lit. ...*Persecutor*
Foo Chih, Chinese...*Ax and skewer*

> *This seems to represent the beast of the book of revelation; It is usually drawn as a sort of beast which comes out of a sea*

Perets—Decan of Taleh

Perseus, Perets, Hebrew- *Breaker*
Perseus et Caput Medusae...anc. Semitic...*Breaker of the head of medusa*
Perseus, Heb....*Breaker, also the Champion*
Rescuer, Modern....*Rescuer of Andromeda*
Victor Gorgonei monstri, Latin...*Victorious over the monster*
Hamil Ra's al Ghul, Arabic...*Carrier of the evil head*
Almirazgual, Spain, Moorish.....*same as above*
Portans caput larvae, Latin, Ulug Beigh transl...*Carrier of the beheaded's brood*
Khem, Egypt...*Holder of the seperated's posterity*

Alpha 2.1 bright lilac and ashy on
chest, breast plate of figure

Mirfak, Hebrew...tr. ....*who assists out of Pleiades (7
sisters, or churches)*
Marfik al Thurayya, Arabic.... *Assister (rescuer) of the
Pleiades*
Mughammid, or Muliammir al Thurayya, Arabic...*the
Concealer of the Pleiades (7 sisters, or churches)* see Rev.
Ch. 1

Beta - spectroscopic binary and variable, 2.3 to
3.5. ...white usually on face of the medusa head

A dark object was found to be orbiting this star and is
thought to be larger than the star it orbits.

Ra's al Ghul, Arabic...*the demons head, mischief maker*
Rosh ha Satan, Hebrew...*satan's head (adversary's)*
Tseih She, Chinese...*the piled up corpses*
Gorgoneum Caput, Vitruvius... *the monsters head*

Gamma.
* Usually lettered Gamma

Al Genib, Arabic...*who carries away (*shown in Gamma
on the right shoulder)

Eta double 5 and 8.5 orange and
smalt blue on raised elbow

Tien Chuen, Chinese...*Heaven's ship*

On the raised wrist holding the sword... is a double
cluster just above Eta Perseus (heavens ship).

Misam al Thurayya, Arabic...*armies (of) the Pleiades...*
Foo Shay, China....*releasing captives*
This is also known as the sword hand of Perseus. It is in this area the *Perseids meteor shower* diverge from the middle of July to the middle of August.

Iota, Zeta, Phi, and Nu...
Make up the sword of Perseus

.Xi 4.5 on lower stepping leg

Mankib al Thurayya, Arabic...lit. *Outpouring Might.... of the Pleiades*

Omicron double 4, and 9, on left foot

Ati, Atik, unknown...lit. *signal of marching expansion,(expedition) - held*
Al Atik, Arabic... (once on the shoulder area) lit. *the signal of the expansion(expedition)held.*

Pi, on the head of medusae in an eye

Al Oneh, Arabic... lit. *genocide exposed*

This sign represents a warrior springing out of the churches or Christian nations (7 sisters) in defense of God's people, (who assists) yet having a problem in that it brings in that defeated leader's brood or head into its realm, as if it were tamed, and as will be shown will suffer because of it.

The name Thurayya in Arabic represents what are called the Pleiades, or 7 sisters from before the Christian era.

Perseus is that strong army of the Lord
which has freed the Andro-meda, and
fights for her, even into modern times.

Shor, Hebrew/Taurus, Latin

Shor, Shur, Reem, Hebrew...*wild ox, the bull coming*...lit.
crushing the barriers, barricades, or prison walls starting.
Al Thaur, Arabic...*the bull ruling*
Tora, likely Median, Ghau, Gau; Persian...*wild ox*
Tauros, Gk...*the bull*
Taurus, Latin...*the bull*
Vrisha, Sanskrit...*rushing bull*
Ughuz, Turkish...*wild ox*
Isis, Coptic...*who saves mightily*
Apis, Coptic...*who comes*
Hrusa, Bohemian...lit. *persecution vindicated*
Thor, Scandinavian...*thundering*

A wild ox with horns lowered and rushing-facing east
in an enraged state...

'Will the wild ox consent to be your servant, or spend
the night by your feed trough? ...Can you tie the wild ox
(Reem) to a furrow with a rope? Or will he harrow the
valleys for you?' Job 39: 9, 10

The King James 1 text uses the word 'unicorn' ; most
believe this is a mistranslation, since the original Hebrew
translated wild ox or reem.

Drawn as the Aurochs (primeval wild bull thought to
be now extinct).

This was an animal that a Caesar in his day described
as being scarcely smaller than an elephant and known
for its untamable nature.

An aurochs is described in an eyewitness account of a staged animal fight in Dresden 1719—

In the arena..... * *'we found 3 bulls there, and another called Auru Ochb (Aurochs) of prodigious grandeur and size.....there then appeared a lioness, a tiger, and a lion, but none of these did much damage...the former ran to and fro, appearing to be frightened, and the lion calmly lay down during these goings on.'*

*A history of zoological gardens in the west...reaktion books...Baratay, and Fugier.

The 7 churches in Anatolia whom Christ addresses in the 1st chapters of the book of Revelations are laid out geographically in form as the stars that make up the Hyades!

Alpha 1.2 pale rose in the Bulls eye, in the Hyades

Al Dabaran, Al Debaran, Aldebaran, Arabic...*the followers, or what follows after the 7 sisters.*
F. Rolleston has .....*the leader, or leader out of the followers lit. the Congregation begins to increase in might.*
Paha, Persian...*the follower*
Ain a Taur, English...*eye of the bull.*
Nair Al Debaran, Arabic... (*Bright one of the followers*)

Al Debaran is part of the Hyades which 7 stars form the face of the bull.

<u>The Hyades - 7 stars which form the face of the bull</u>

Hyades, Greek...*the congregated*...lit. *– given strength to deliver the persecuted*

Parilicium, Parilic-ium, Latin...trad.-*belonging to the Judge....*lit.
Abundant knowledge of—confidence of deliverance flowing from God

Aleph, Hebrew....trad.-*strong*...lit.- *Strong knowledge of living word in heart*
...In Hindi...trad.-*A temple, or wagon.*

Hyades in China

Yu Shi...*Ruler of the rain...figuratively-Outpouring?*
Tien Lin....*celestial, heavenly public granary ...as a blessing or bounty*
Pal...*a hand net or rabbit net. .....*as *going to capture;* and ...in combination with other local stars *'the announcer of invasion on the border'*
Tien Kaea...*the heavenly street, or Way*
Tien Tsze...*Heavens festival*

Beta 2.1 and 10 brilliant pure white, and pale grey, on the northern horn tip, *same star as gamma aurigae.

El Nath, Semitic...trad.-*the butting one...*lit. *-the expanded congregation's (fish's) powerful protection, guard, military.*
Al Natih, Arabic...trad.-*the butting one. ...*lit. *-the expanded congregation's power signals /extends protection*
Hutab Huj, Hindu...trad. *-devourer of the sacrifice*
Al Karn al Thaur al Shamaliyyah, Arabic...loc. *the northern horn of the bull*

Gamma 4.2 yellow at vortex of the Hyades triangle

Aw Wal Al Dabaran, (Aldabaran) Arabic...trad.-*the first of the followers* Hyadum 1, Gk...*the deliverer's, rescuer's...*

Delta 4.2 on northern line east of gamma

Hyadum 2, Gk...*the deliverer's, liberators*

Epsilon 3.6 near the northern eye opposite Aldebaran.

Ain, Arabic...loc. *the eye*, lit. *powerful reach of multiplied (fish), and/or increase*

Zeta 3.5

Tien Kwan, Chinese...*the heavenly gate*

The Pleiades-7 stars out of which Perseus arises
China.....7 sisters of industry

Pleiades, Gk....trad. ...*congregation of the Judge, or Ruler...from Pliades or Plias Gk....to sail*
Pleiades, Hesiod... described as the *7 virgins, the 7 sisters*
Chima, Kimah, Hebrew...*the accumulation*
Sukkoth R Noth, Heb. Rabbis'....*booths of the maidens, or tents of the daughters*
Kima, Syrian...*a family group, growing*
Al Thurayya, Arabic...*an abundant accumulation*
Al Najm, Arabic...*par excellence*
Vergiliae, Latin...*from 'ver' =spring*
Sifunsterri, Anglo-Saxon...*ready to expand, or multiply, travel*

"I am Alpha and Omega, the first and the last: and, What you see, write in a book, and send it to the 7 churches that are in Asia; unto Ephesus, and unto Smyrna, and unto Pergamos and unto Thyatira, and unto Sardis, and unto Philadelphia, and unto Laodicea." Rev. 1:11

Stars of Pleiades, Arabic

Eta 3.0 greenish yellow in Pleiades

Al Cyone, Arabic...trad. *-the center...*lit. *-the Liberator(s) extend vision/view of the (hidden) multiple lives*
Al Wasat, Arabic...trad. *...the central one...*lit. *...the alliance's powerful crushing sign*
Al Jauz, or Al Jauzah Al Nair, Arabic...trad.*The bright one/ The Branch, (es)...*lit. *military might increases....Al Nair...*lit.- *expedition's begin.*

It is out of this group that Perseus (the breaker of Andro-Meda's bonds) sprang forth.

Pleiades/fl= Flamsteeds location catalogue number.

Maia, May, Maja, Magnus, or Maou...4.o fl 20 *Outpouring help-outreaches*
Electa, Electra, ...4.6 fl 17 *elect*
Merope...5 silvery white...fl 23 *prophetic visions*
Taygete, and Taygeta....double 5.1 and 10 lucid white and violet fl19 *strength to help/save*
Celaeno, or Celeno...6.5 silvery white...fl 16 *the delivered increase, converted*
Sterope-1 and 2...6.5 and 7...fl 21 and 22 *faithful to the end*

Atlas...fl 27 and Pleione-fl 28 were modern additions, added in Riccioli's day... not found named of the 7 in antiquity. They form the end of the handle of the Pleiad dipper. (Pleione was named after the whole). Sometimes they are categorized as having a paternal and maternal representation of the asterism Pleiades. The original names may have been misplaced in history.

This constellation seems to have all the attributes of a coming judgment. A justice or recompense in defense of and including the participation of the 7 sisters or church....forewarned, and proclaimed.

In a literal sense a military action may also be interpreted here...one which defends the Judeo-Christian camps, or nations. This is the asterism out of which Perseus, the breaker of the bonds, and rescuer of Andro-Meda leaps forth.

Al Cyone, Al Wasat, and Al Jauz all names for eta Taurus of the asterism Pleiades may be describing the end of WWII in a literal sense, at least the Church armed in defense.

This sign represents the church armed at home
and in defense of those oppressed abroad.
Especially during the great war and ww2.

K'Sil—Decan of Shor

K'sil, Chesil, Hebrew....*warrior, the bound together -alliance*
Gibbor, Hebrew....*the giant*
Al Jabbar, Arabic....*the giant*
Uru-Ki, Akkadian...*the Light of the earth*
Orion, Semitic...F. Rolleston...*coming forth as light*
Gigas, Latin...*the giant*
Al Babadur, Arabic...*the strong one*
Al Jauzah, Arabic....*the Branch's house*

Alpha irregular variable .7 orange on right shoulder (eastern side)

Ibt Al Jauzah, Arabic....lit.-*reaching home sign of (the Branch) (es)(military)*
Betelgeuze, trad...*house of the Branch...(Judah, Israel, Church)*
Besn, Persian...lit. *home-body-lives (with) decimated-numbers*
Claria, Coptic...lit. *increased strength, new beginning*

'I am the vine, you are the branches'. Jn. 15:5

Beta -double .3 and 8 bluish- white on raised foot

Rai Al Jauzah, Arabic-Al Sufi....lit. ...*Lord's Power extended to...Al Jauzah (the Branches) (military)*
Rijl Jauzah Al Yusra, Arabic...*herdsmen of the Branch*
Rigel, Rigol, Semitic trad. ... F. Rolleston -*who treads underfoot*
Al Najid, Arabic...*the conquerer*

Gamma -slightly variable 2.0 pale
yellow on west arm or shoulder

Bellatrix, Semitic traditional...F. Rolleston...*hastily coming*
Al Murzam Al Najid, Arabic...Uleg Beigh...*the roaring conqueror, or the conquering lion.....F. Rolleston...the prince*
Al Ruzam, Arabic, Al Sufi...trad.-*the Lion*

England is seen as a lion...the British lion, and it's offspring are considered by most scholars the young lions as shown in a future military event in Ezekiel 38- which equate to the US, Australia, Canada, etc. Since the return of the Lord has not happened at this point in the story, this must equate to the Christian nations of the west, hence branches and not The Branch/ Christ as yet.

Orion's belt asterism names

Chinese ...*a weighing beam*
Al Mizan al Hakk, Arabic ...the *accurate scale-beam*

(Justice seems to be represented here)

Delta - double and slightly variable 2.4 and 6.8 bright white and pale violet westernmost star of Orion's belt

Mintaka...Semitic trad, F. Rolleston... *dividing the belt*
Al Mintakah, Arabic, trad. ... *the belt* lit. *they reach the hidden stronghold /prison*

Epsilon- 1.8 bright white on center of belt
middle star in Orion's belt.

Al Natham, Al Nathm, Arabic, trad. ... *string of pearls, bullions*
Al Nilam, Arabic...lit. *giving instruction to migrate/ pour out*

Zeta- triple 2.5, 6.5, and 9
topaz yellow, light purple and grey

Yellow -identification star, purple-royalty the King's people, grey –ashes
Al Nitak, Arabic, trad. ...*girded about,* lit. *...end of imprisonment of the hidden* F. Rolleston lit. ...*the wounded*

This is the location of a group of nebulae, exploding *stars The appearance is like a burning bush, with a red mist spilling out almost resembling a faint cross with a*

figure on it....down to the foot of the cross where what appears to be a scorpions stinger striking at the lower part of it....it also resembles a dark horse - neck and head silhouetted over a red mist. M 42, M 43, Barnard 33

This asterism of (Orion's belt) seems to represent a military justice....with the memory of those who suffered before them girded about them (the wounded) -Zeta Orion. And if shown as a scale, the wound shows to be heavy and weighing down the eastern side of the beam. Don't ever forget the holocaust.

<u>on the sword of Orion</u>
Eta triple 3.5, 5, and 5

Saiph, Semitic, trad. -F. Rolleston ...*bruised in the foot,* lit...*crushing power reaches those promoting imprisonment or separation*
Saiph al Jabbar, Arabic...*the sword of the giant*
Al Alkat, Arabic...*the golden grains (wheat), or spangles...* lit. ...*the mighty learn and hold power to finish/ end*

Theta 4.6 pale white
Marks the 'fish-mouth' (scabbard,
sheath) part of the sword

Trapezium, Latin...though typically unnamed. Named for a 4 sided table centuries ago when only 4 stars were visible.
But at least six stars are found in this area known as the trapezium. *"The great nebula", or Orion's' Nebulae, and it appears as a huge bright yellow-orange explosion*

Iota triple and nebulous 3.5, 8 and 11
Near tip of sword
White, pale blue, and grape red

*Colors of the US, England, and France

Nair al Saif, Arabic-Al Tisane...*the bright one of the sword*
Fa, China...*a middleman, punishment*...lit. *connected, and/or fixed with power.*
Tui, or Jui, China...*the sharp edge*

Kappa 2.4 on right leg

Rijl Jauzah al Yamna, Arabic....loc. ... *right leg of the branches-*
lit. *expanding expedition ...branch(es) strengthened –*

Lambda double 3.8 and 6 pale white and violet,
on head of Orion

Al Ras Al Jauzah, Arabic...trad. ...*head of the branch(es)*
Meissa, Semitic...*coming forth*
Aryika, Hindi....*honorable, or worthy*
Invaka, Hindi...*given strength of hand*
Al Hak'ah, Arabic...*the bounty hunter*
Al Maisan, Arabic...*the recipient of overwhelming power*
Al Tahayi, Arabic- Al Sufi...*the stronghold of those extending help*

Nu 4.7 and Xi 4.6
on raised hand holding club

Shwuy Foo, Chinese...*a well, or watering place*

Nu, and Xi, on hand grasping staff or club...marks the radiant point of the meteor stream the Orionids of the 18th of October, (similar to the location around the sword of Perseus for the Perseoid meteor showers of the summer.)

Nu, Xi, with Chi 1 and 2, mark the outline of the pounding club which begins where the lower horn of Taurus ends in a point.

Omicron 1, 2 Pi 1, 2, and 3,4,5,6
on the lion's skin

Al Taj, Persia- Al Tizini...*the crown...* lit. ...*the signs strong reach.*
Al Kumm, Arabic, loc. ... *the sleeve or garment-* lit. ...*the hold connected to the flow, stream's influx*
Al Dhawaib, Arabic-Uleg Beigh...*pendant*
Manica, Latin- Al Sufi.... *a protecting gauntlet*

Tau 3.6
just north of Rigel (beta Orion)

Yuh Tsing, China...*the golden well*

Upsilon 4.7
on lower edge of tunic or garment left thigh raised

Thabit, Arabic-... *endurer* ...F. Rolleston...*treading on*

Other names associated with Orion.

Al Rai, Arabic...lit. *The Great Shepherd...or the Mighty Arm of the Lord, far reaching Lord*
Nux, Hebrew....trad. *the strong*

Heka, Chaldean...trad. *coming, bringing*
Niphla, Chaldean....trad. *the mighty*

This is the Lord's warrior rising up delivering his chosen people, and establishing them in their land with justice.

A foreshadow of this was Cyrus the Persian cir. 500 BC. However this story in the sky is a calendar of prophecy which begins at the birth of the Messiah 500 years after Cyrus.

This constellation seems to represent the events surrounding or at least starting around the world war's especially ww2

Eridanus—Decan of Shor

Eridanus, Heb. ...*river of the judge*
Aria-dan, Akkadian....*the strong river*
Eridan-us, Hebrew, Latin...*Strong river, connected to judgment*
Al Nair, Nar or Nahar, Arabic...*the river*
...sometimes Nahal, same as *Nile*
Guad, Moors...*similar to Arabic 'wadi'- river*
Guadalquivir, Spanish....*the river of the...'quivir' arrows or judgment...*
Wadi Al Kabir, Arabic...*the great river*
D' Potamos, Greek....*the river*
Eridanos, Greek...*a river*
Melas, Gk. La Lande...*black,* Melo, Latin...*black*
Khem, Coptic...*black*
Eridan, French -Eridano, Italian-Fluss Eridanus, German...*strong river*

Alpha .4 white,
down near the South Pole

Al Aliir al Nahr, Arabic...trad. *the end of the river*
Achernar....same as above F. Rolleston- *latter part of the river*
Shwuy Wei, Chinese...*devouring isolation...hades?*

Beta 2.9 topaz yellow,
3 degrees northwest of Orion's foot

Al Kursiyy al Jauzah, Arabic...*footstool, (of the Branch(es).*
Cursa, Semitic-F. Rolleston... *bent down,* lit. *judgment starts*

Gamma 3.0
corner after first drop south of the river

Zaurac, Zaurak, Semitic...lit. *judgment*
Al Nair al Zaurak, Arabic...lit. *river of judgment (the Judge)*

Eta 3.7 pale yellow,
at 10 degrees below the celestial equator
where the river takes a dramatic turn downwards

Azha, Semitic- Al Sufi-lit. ...*strongly separated, abandoned*
Ashiyane, Persian...same as above
Al Udhiyy, Arabic- Kazwini-trad. ...*ostrich's eggs (nest?)*

From eta down to tau (-10 degrees to -23 degrees below the celestial equator) is where (beast of the sea) Ketus' bear like paws and breast merge with the river of the judge. This area was set apart by Al Sufi as 'Al Sadr al Ketus' or, the breast of the beast of the sea.

Theta double 3 and 5.25,
down at 40 degrees below the celestial equator.

Al Thalim, Arabic, Uleg Beigh-trad. ...*the ostrich (a flightless bird that hides its head, and is careless with its young)*
lit. ...*guarding, (hiding, shielding) powerful knowledge reaching outward. Ignoring reality*
Hyde has ....*a dam, as something clogging up the river*

Omicron 1- 4.1 clear white, 8 degrees north-east
of Gamma Eridanus on upper part of river

Al Baid, Arabic-trad. ...*the egg in the nest, incubating,*
Beid, Semitic...*incubating*

Omicron 2- triple 4, 9.1, and 10.8 orange
and sky blue just below Omicron 1

Al Kaid, Arabic-trad. ...*the egg shells -as thrown out from the nest closeby, chicks of the ostrich*

Tau 2 -4.0 yellow
at turn of river below Ketus' paws.

Al Hinayat al Nahr, Arabic-trad. *the bend in the river*
Al Anchat al Nahr, Arabic...lit. *river of multiple stillborn... (abortion?)*

Upsilon 1- Upsilon 7, at 30 degrees below the celestial equator turning another direction towards the south.

Bamma'yim, Hebrew...*in the water*
Theemin, Semitic-F. Rolleston ...*the water (in)*

Other names in Eridanus

Phaet, Semitic-F. Rolleston...*mouth (of the river)*
Ozha, Semitic...F. Rolleston...*going forth*

It would seem the Ostrich's brood is attached to this river. *Some of its known characteristics are...*

As an animal that is careless for its young, sometimes crushing them, and also for putting its head in the sand, (Re- Truth?)

These traditions, concepts are aggressively guarded and held by the Ketus (sea beast). Those unwilling to see the truth, (bible, Gospel, revelations of God, and just simple facts of reality) with the added shame of abortion, and/or using children irresponsibly...

putting them in harm's way. This sounds familiar, and it is a dangerous river.

Names such as 'black' suggest the type of river, and it's association with darkness, without light, what the beast of the sea holds to, and it's direction to the nether regions mostly unknown and unseen, but in the furthest reaches south. This paints a bleak picture of its characteristics, but nonetheless seems right on target.

This is a river of judgment, or justice.

Aurignac—Decan of Shor

Aurignac, Hebrew...*the Shepherd*
Auriga, Unknown...*the Charioteer or Wagoneer*
Al Rakib, Arabic...*the Driver*
Eniochoz, Gk...*the Rein-holder*...notice similarity to name *Enoch*

Heniochus, Latin...*Holder of the reins*
Al Dhu al Inan, Arabic-trad. ...*The Rein holder.*
Cocher, French—Cocchiere, Italian...*Coachman -Holder of the reins*
Woo Chay, Chinese...*five chariots*
Wainman, Semitic...*Wagon-driver*
Al Masik al Inan, Arabic...*Holder of the bridle*
Pastor, Rabbi Aben Ezra...*Shepherd*
Fuhrman, German...*One who steers the boat*

Alpha .3 white
held in the Shepherd's lap

Alioth, Hebrew, *She-goat...lit. Strong know extended vision of protection*
Dil-gan-I-ku, Akkadian...*the messenger of light's leader*
I-ku, Assyria...*the leader*
Al Anz, Arabic...*the mighty perpetually warring*
Amaltheiaz Keraz, Gk transl. of Semitic...*Gods' fold, remnant armed*
Amalthea, Semitic...*God's fold...*
Cornu copiae, Latin...*horn of plenty*
Capra, Latin....*a female goat*
Cabrilla, Spain...*a goat, in the feminine*
Capella, Latin...*she-goat*
Chevre, France...*goat*
Kinesai Cheimonaz, Gk-Aratos...*little she-goat*

Beta 2.1 lucid yellow
on the right shoulder (eastern) of the Rein-holder

Al Mankib dhi'l Inan, Arabic-loc. ...*the shoulder of the rein-holder,*
Or, loc+lit....*the shoulder of ; seeing beginning*

Gamma 2.1 brilliant white
on eastern, or right heel
(identical with Al Nath, Beta Tauri)

Al Ka'b dhi'l Inan, Arabic....*the heel of the Rein-holder*
Ayyuk, Aiyuk, Semitic-F. Rolleston...*wounded in the foot*
Al Tawabi al Ayyuk, Arabic-trad. ...*the she-goats' attendants*

Delta 4.1 yellow
on head of the rein holder

Praja-pati, Hindu...*Lord of created beings*...lit. the *Word of the Lord conceives or multiplies*

Epsilon variable 3 to 4.5
on arm holding Capella and young...

Al Anz, Arabic-lit. ...*the powerful unseen warrior*

Zeta 4.0 orange
The area of the kids, or offspring

Agni, Albumaser-Arabic...*the Lambs*
Capellae, Latin-Bayer transl....*Capella's offspring*
Eriphoi, Greek...*kids*
Haedi, Latin...*kids*

Iota 3.1 on western or left foot

Also, same name as Gamma Auriga
Al Tawabi al Ayyuk, Arabic-Al Kazwini....*The she-goats attendants*...lit. *The mighty help the remnants reach home*

Lambda double 5 and 9.5

Pale yellow and plum color; Mu, 5.1; and Sigma 5.3
in center of figure

Al H' iba, Arabic...*the tent, covering* -lit. ...*the separated reach home*
Tseen Hwang, Chinese....*the heavenly pool*

This seems to be the remnant of Israel returning home, as the goat represents rejected, mistreated, same as in Gedi (Capricorn), where the Messiah was rejected of men. Isaiah 53

Thaumin, Hebrew/Gemini, Latin

Thaumin, and Teomin, Hebrew...*the twins*
Al Tau'aman, Arabic...*the twins*
Mas-mas, Assyrian...*the twins*
Mithuna, Hindi...*boy and girl*
Gemini, Latin....*twins*
Gemelli, Italian...twins, Gemeaux, French...*twins*
Ge Twisan, Anglo Saxon...*the twins*
Didymoi, Didumoi, Greek...*twins*
Du Paikar, or Do Patkar, Persian...*the two figures*
Frere, Anglo Norman...*United beginning life's reunion*
'The twins were placed in the sky by Jove, in reward for their brotherly love so strongly manifested while on earth'.....Richard Allen Hinckley 'Star names....'...from Manlius' writings...showing an early understanding not far removed from the prophetic meaning. This is the rapture of the church to meet the Lord in the air. This also represents the marriage supper...see Alpha, and Delta Gemini

Alpha binary 2.7, and 3.7 bright white and
pale white on the head of the upper figure,
the feminine one with harp and arrows.

Castor, anc. Semitic...*Mortal one of the twins.* F Rolleston...
Ruler, haste
Apellon, Doric...*Mighty call (shout) living seeing unseen.*
(rapture)
Punarvarsu, Indus 5th nakshatra....*the Two Good Again...*
(reconciled)

Beta 1.1 orange
on head of the lower figure resting with club at side

Pollux, Polluces, Greek....from Poludeuzes... *the Immortal*
of the twins
Hrakles, Gk...*same as Hercules, or Herakles, bruiser, see*
constellation of same name. This represents the same
individual.
Al Ras al Jauzah, Arabic... *the head of the branch(es)*
Ketpholtsuman, unknown origin...

Gamma 2.2 brilliant white in foot of Pollux

Al Maisan, Arabic... *the Marching One*
Elhenaat, Riccioli; or
Al Henah, Arabic...*the marked, or the brand...*F. Rolleston
has ... *hurt, afflicted*
(bruised in the foot)

Delta double 3.8 and 8 pale white and purple
on elbow of Castor

Just north of delta here is the radiant point of the
Geminid meteor stream visible in early October.

Al Wasat, Arabic....*the center, or middle*
Ta Tsun, China...*the great wine-jar*
Wasat, Wesat, Semitic...*central*

Epsilon double 3.4 and 9.5 bright white and cerulean
blue - on hem of Castor's tunic...on right knee

Mebsuta, Semitic-F. Rolleston trnsl. ...*treading underfoot*
Al Mabsutat, Arabic....*the outstretched (paw of lion)*

Zeta variable 3.7 to 4.5 pale topaz-
left knee of Pollux

Al Makbuda, Arabic....*the contracted (paw of lion)*
Mekbuda, Semitic...lit. *many bodies delivered strongly*

*Epsilon and Zeta reveal a movement of the lions' paw
toward the mortal ones (church), and contract back to
the immortal one (Christ the Lion).

Eta binary and variable 3.2 to 3.7, and 9
in front of Castors left foot.

Tejat prior, Semitic...*sign of the living's strong finish*
Yue, Chinese...*a battle ax (as set aside for the moment)*
Propous, Propos, Propus, Semitic...lit. *many/ much talk
–(Lord recognized, the pierced)*
Al Tahayi, Arabic...lit. *departed reach (dead in Christ rise
first)*

Mu double 3.2 and 11 crocus yellow and blue
on left heel of Castor

Tejat posterior, Semitic...*sign of the living's strong finish*
Nuhatai, Semitic...*Fish (church) multiplied and separated
a sign*

Pish Pai, Semitic...*word-news that death conquered, word spreads*
Calx, Tycho's catalogue...*the heel*

Chi 5.0

Tseih Tsing, China...*piled up fuel*

This sign seems to be speaking of the rapture of the church prior to the war at Ar Megiddo- in the valley of Megiddo. Castor representing the church, and Pollux represents the Messiah. As well the weapons of the Lord and his church are set aside for the moment, possibly in lieu of the beginning of the marriage supper.

Arnebo—Decan of Thaumin

Arnebo, Arnebeth, Hebrew...*enemy of Him that comes*
Al Arnab, Arabic...*the enemy*
Bashti-Beki, Egypt....*Offender confounded*
Al Kursiyy al Jabbar, Arabic...*the bent down of the giant (Orion)*
Lepus, Latin...*The hare, eared, rough footed, lightfooted, swift.*
Lebre, Port. -Lepre, Ita. -Lievre, Fr. -Hase, Ger.-*the hare*

Alpha double 2.7 and 9.5 pale yellow and gray
on right shoulder of the hare

Arsh, century dict. Semitic...*murderer*
Arneb, Arabic, Semitic...*enemy*

Beta double 3.5 and 11 deep yellow and blue
on right elbow of hare

Nibal, Burritt...*deception*
Nibal, Hebrew...*the mad*
Nihal, Semitic... *given to imprisonment*

Gamma
on right foot of hare

Rakis, Unknown....*bound*

Delta

Sugia, Semitic....*deceiver*

'The Dendera planisphere has in its place a serpent apparently attacked by some bird of prey'.

'The constellation Lepus sets soon after the rising of Corvus.

'The Bantus' of Africa ...connected...in a story, asserting that the hare, ill treated by the moon (symbolic of the church), scratched her face and we still see the scratches.'

This seems to represent the times following the end of the cold war, which was a thawing of the 2 great wars ww1 and 2.

The enemy is that which feels slighted by the church.

The common theme of the Crusades centuries after the fact in nations opposed to Christianity to stir up opposition, and anger against the west is a type of this 'slight' based on the manipulation of half-truths which the serpent uses.

This figure interestingly enough has it's head drawn in the very same shape and angle as what has been shown as the modern hand signal for 'peace'. Fraudful in that the same people use the symbol of the inverted broken cross in a circle for the 'peace' sign, when it represented Christian persecution in Nero's time.

A hare is also a creature which hides in holes and rocks and multiplies.

This figure may represent the target of a modern crusade such as the recent war on terror which was to capture or imprison the enemy of Israel's freedom, and the freedoms of the Christian west. This could represent 'Anarchists and terrorists' which can multiply rapidly (by lies) as a hare. The Latin suggests 'rough footed'.

Abur—Decan of Thaumin

Abur, Hebrew...*Mighty*
Al Habor, Arabic...*the Mighty*
Al Shira Al Jemeniya....*the chief of the right hand*
Sier, Egypt...*the prince*
Sierios Megas, Gk.....*major prince*
Canis Major, Latin...*large canine, greater hound*
Al Kalb al Jabbar, Arabic....*the hound (ing) of the Giant*
Al Kalb al Akbar, Arabic....*the hound (ing) of the Great*

Alpha binary 1.43 and 8.5 brilliant white
and yellow on the hounds' snout

Sirius, Syrius, Hebrew...*princely, scorching*
Nazir (Aschere), Semitic...*the prince who shall come*
Al Shira or Al Sira, Arabic...*the prince*

Al Abur al Yamaniyyah, Arabic...*the mighty of the right hand in the south*
Prooptes, Plutarch, Gk...*the Leader*
Tseen Lang, China... *the heavenly wolf*
Hannabeah, Phoenician...*the barker*
Syr, Celtic...*the noble*

Beta 2.3 white
on right paw reaching upwards

Al Murzim, Arabic....*the announcer*
Murzim, Mirzam, Semitic...*announcement*

Gamma 4.5
on jaw of hound

Muliphen, Semitic...*exortations*
Mirza, Century atlas...*war preparations*

Delta 2.2 light yellow
on midsection of hound

Al Wazn, Arabic...*weight*
Wezen, Semitic...*warriors*

Epsilon double 2 and 9 pale orange and violet
on right rear knee of hound

Al Adhara, Arabic...*the virgins*
Adara, Semitic...*pure*

Zeta 3.0 light orange
on raised rear left foot

Al Furud, Arabic...*the bright single ones*
Furud, Semitic...*connected to deliverance*

Eta 2.4 pale red
on tail of hound

Aludra, Semitic...*newly freed*
Al Adhara, Arabic...*the virgins*

This seems to represent that which chases (the hare) the enemy of freedom and Christianity. A powerful nation a mighty nation of the right hand...(Christ)...the announcement may represent the recent coalition to fight global terrorism.

Sebak—Decan of Thaumin

Sebak, Semitic...*victorious*
Al Kalb al Mutakaddim, Arabic...*the preceeding dog*
Al Kalb al Asghar, Arabic...*the lesser dog*
Canis Minor, Latin...*the smaller hound*
Il Cane Minore, Italian...*the lesser dog*
Le Petit Chien, French...*the little dog*
Der Kleine Hund, German...*the little hound*

Alpha binary .4 and 13 yellowish white, and yellow
on dogs belly

Procyon, Hebrew...*preceeding dog, early, Redeemer*
Prokyon, *Gk...preceeding, Redeemer...preceeding the Redeemer*
Antecanis, Latin...*preceeding hound*
Al Shira al Shamiyya *or* Shemelliya, Arabic....*the chief of the rising up...north*
Kakkab Paldara, Euphratean... *the crossing of the water-dog, (river of heaven)*

Pur Cahen, Egyptian...lit. *speaking of the deliverance from death*

Beta 3.5 white
on shoulder or collar area of little dog

Al Gomeisa, Arabic-Semitic...*burdened, loaded, bearing for others*
Ghumaisa, Semitic...*watery eyed, weeping one*
Al Murzim, Arabic...*announcer, prince-ruler*

Zeta, theta, omicron, and pi

Shwuy Wei, China...*a place of water*

This seems to be representing the rapture of the church, and the meeting in the air; the overcomers.

Also a sort of announcement or realization to the world that this precedes the return of the Lord. The enemy would gather together his armies to fight against the Lord at Armageddon, this sign may be what makes him realize that the Lord is returning just as He and His people have said.

Sartan, Hebrew/Cancer, Latin

Sartan, Hebrew-trad. ...*who holds*
Al Sartan, Arabic...*same as above*
Sartano, Syriac...*same as above*
Kahn-ker, cer, unknown origin....*resting places of travelers, -circled, embraced...with arms protected.*
Karkios, Greek...*the crab*
Cancer, Latin...*a crab*

Klaria, Coptic...*the cattle folds*
Scarabeaus, anc. Egypt...*a certain type of beetle*
Karka, Carcatta, Carcallacam, Sanscrit...*to encircle*
Sidhaya, Sanskrit...*prosperous*
Kui Hia, Chinese....*great crab*
Nepa, unknown origin...*Crab*

Alpha 4.4 and 11 white and red on left, lower claw arm

Al Susannah, Arabic-trad. ...*the claws-* lit. ...*the purchased*
Acubene, Semitic...*the sheltering*

Beta 4.0 on southern foot

Al Tarff, Arabic...*the end*

Gamma 4.6, and Delta 4.3
straw color in center of figure ...
Delta the lower one is on the solar ecliptic line

Asellus borealis, and Ascellus australis....*north and south she colts, donkeys*

Epsilon faint star cluster between gamma and delta

Praesepe, Semitic roots...*multitude, offspring, innumerable*
Praesaepe, Latin...*cradle, crib...*
Pesebre, Spanish...*same as above*
Ermelia, Coptic...*nursing, nourishing*

Zeta   ternary 5.6, 6.3, and 6 yellow, orange,
yellowish...changing /on rear shell

Tegmen, Tegmine, unknown origin... trad. *the shell / protection*

Other names

Tsew Ke, China...a wine flagon (grouped with xi, and omega Leo, and kappa and xi Cancer)

This may represent both those *added* to meet the Lord in the air; tribulation martyrs-as well as those who recognize His coming to earth any moment as they witness Him in the clouds, IE Waiting for him. Those who mourn their King whom they had pierced.

The Lord and church in coming as a circle from heaven...(Arx) The meeting in the air visible to those on earth, (Ash) and those coming to him from out of the earth, (Argo).

The accumulation of names in this suggest a protected group embraced near the end; both in the heavens, and on earth. The Marriage supper in the heavenlies, simultaneously the tribulation period on earth written of in the bible.

Arx—Decan of Sartan

Arx, Semitic... *the lesser fold, bier*
Rukub, Chaldean, Kassite...*a vehicle*
Rukhubh, Hebrew...*a wain*
Al Dubb al Asghar, Arabic...*the fold's procession*
Dobher, Phoenicia...*the fold*
Al Rakabah or Rukkabah, Arabic....*the riders*
Banat al Na'ash al Sughra, Arabic...*daughters of the lesser bier.*
Bier, Arabia...*a procession*
Arcas, Arctos, Greek...*travellers*
Litli Vagn, Danish...*little wagon, smaller chariot.*
Maidens, the 7 stars, modern English, ...*same as Pleiades*

Ursa Minor, Latin. *Erroneously named. Some confusion took root when the original word 'Bier'...as in 'a procession' was transformed into 'Bear'.

More recent depictions closely resemble a badger, a smallish yet ferocious creature able to drive off much larger competitors and adversaries. Honey badgers are near immune to snake venom. They will sleep for a few moments if bitten, and are voracious snake hunters. This is used to identify location.

The wagon or chariot procession is the consensus in ancient times.

Alpha double2.2, 9.5 topaz yellow-pale white on tip of badger's tail, or first- lead star of the chariot

Polus, Greek...*similar name to Pollux of Gemini*
Polaris, modern....*pole star, Leader of the procession*
Ti Tao, China...*the Emperors seat*
Pih Keih, Ta Shin, and
Tien Hwang Ta Ti, China....*the Great Imperial (Kingly) Ruler of Heaven*
Al Kutb Al Shamaliyy, Arabic...*northern axle, spindle*
Al Kaukab al Shamaliyy, Arabic...*the star of the north*
Mismal, Syrian-Damascus...*needle, or nail*
Yilduz, Turkey...*the star par excellence* This is the star whose light was concealed for a time after the Ottomans capture of Constantinople.*
Al Kiblah, Arabic...*the direction, Director*

This is the star which displaced Thuban (Alpha Draco) in a prior era as marking the north celestial pole due to the precession over millenia.

Beta 2.0 reddish top rear of chariot or wagon

Kochab, Hebrew...*waiting on (serving) Him who comes*
Anwar al Farkadain, Arabic...*the light of the calves*
Guadare, Spanish...*beholding*
Nair al Farkadain, Arabic...*the bright one of the calves*

Gamma 1and, 2 3.3, 5.8 bottom
rear of chariot or wagon

Vigiles, Riccioli...*the vigilant, guards*
Alifa al Farkadain, Arabic...*the dim one of the 2 calves*
(seen as one in Arabia)
Pherkad major, Pherkad minor, Semitic...*major and minor*
calf

Delta 4.3 greenish next from alpha

Chioreuths proth, and deutera, Greek...*first and second*
dancers

Zeta 4.3 flushed white at junction of chariot and reigns,

Kow Chin, China...*having been saved from death*

Lower case b...5th magnitude

How Kung, China...*the empress*

7 principle stars, 24 in total. This is a reflection of
the 7 churches addressed in Revelations, and as well
the 24 elders described there. In revelations Christ
held 7 stars in His right hand in John's vision. The 24
elders represents 24 patriarchs 12 of which may be the
Apostles of Christ. This is the same figure as Pleiades,
but magnified and defined. The next sign defines them

further. Another theme in this sign is the dancing. The celebration in the heavens.

The church that was gone before, Apostles and Patriarchs, and the Leader of the procession being Christ Himself. Could represent the Messianic Jews and Israelis...the foundational representatives of the church with Christ.

Ash—Decan of Sartan

Ash, Ayish, Semitic...*a bier, (procession) the greater bier, fold*
Dobh, the latter Dobh, Hebrew...*the fold*
Bier, Syria...*procession*
Banat Na'ash al Kubra, Arabic...*the daughters of the great bier...mourners*
Arthurs chariot, Angles-English...*(Arthur is the same as Arcturus)*
Wagen, Wain, Teutonic...*a wagon, or chariot*
Ajala, Aben Ezra...*wagon*
Wain, Gk... *wagon*
Plaustrum, Latin...*wagon or cart*
Cataletto, Italian...*a bier*
Chalitsa, Kalitsa, Phoenicia...*same as Calisto of Pleiades*
Stori Vagn, Scandinavian...*the great wagon*
Woz Niebeski, Polish...*heavenly wain*
Tseih Sing, China...*the 7 stars (known as the government)* (7 churches in Rev.1)
Saptar Shaya, India... *the 7 anchorites* (see above)
Himmelwagen, German ...*way to Heaven*
Irmines Wagen, Saxon...*noble wagen*
*Ursa Major, Latin...same *as is Ursa Minor translated bear instead of bier*

Alpha 2 and 11 yellow top rear of
chariot or wagon square

Dubb, Dubhe, Semitic...*the fold*
Thahr al Dubb al Akbar, Arabic...*the back of the greater
fold*

Beta 2.5 greenish white bottom
rear of the wagon square

Al Marakk, Arabic...*the loins (of the fold)*
Mirak, Semitic...*loins* lit. *multitudes reach for Lord's
strong hand /hold*

Gamma 2, 5 topaz
bottom front of wagon square

Al Falidh, Arabic...*thigh*
Phacad, Phecda... *guarded, numbered*

Delta 3.6 pale yellow top front of wagon square

Megrez, Semitic....*given strength*
Kwan, Tien Kuen, China...*heavenly authority*

Epsilon 2.1 east of delta point

Alioth, Hebrew...*ewe, or she goat*
Al Hawar, Arabic...*bright white*

Zeta double 2.1, 4.2 brilliant white,
pale emerald eastward of epsilon

Anak al Banat, Arabic...*the necks of the maidens (in ref.
to the mourners of the bier)*

Eta 1.9 brilliant white easternmost
point of constellation

Alcaid, Al Kaid, Arabic...*the assembled*
Kaid Banat al Na'ash, Arabic...*governor of the daughters
of the bier, chief of the mourners*

Theta double 3.4 combined brilliant white
southwest of beta west below the chariot

Sarir Banat al Na'ash, Arabic...*the throne of the mourners*
(with t,h,u,phi,e,f)
Thufr al Ghizlan, Arabic...*the gazelles' tracks, or path*
Wan Chang, China...*the Literary Illumination..(Light of
the Word)*

Iota binary 3.2 and 13 topaz yellow and purple
Kappa 3.5

Al Phikra al Thalitha, Arabic-Ulug Beg...*the 3rd spring
(leap) of the daughters*

Lambda 3.7 and Mu 3.2 red

Al Kafzah al Thaniyah, Arabic...together, *the 2nd spring
(leap) of the daughters....* It seems the Arabians illustrated
this constellation as a gazelle representing the daughters
of the procession.
Tania, Heb...*daughters*
Tania borealis, and australis...*north and south/ daughters*
Chung Tae, China...*middle dignitary*

Nu double 3.5 and 12 orange and cerulean blue and Xi binary 3.9 and 5.5 subdued white and grayish white

Al Ula, Arabic...*the first spring (leap) (nu)*
Al Fikrah al Ula, Arabic-Ulug Beg...lit. *bright one of the teachers*
Hea Tae, China...*lower dignitary*

Sigma 5.2, Sigma 2 4.8 and 9.5
flushed white and sapphire

Al Thiba, Arabic...*guarded reach home*

The theme here seems to be (what) a bier, wain, or procession (who) of the fold.

Shown as a gazelle following toward -turning toward Arcturus, English Arthur...the 2nd decan of Bethulah the Virgin. These are the followers of The Highest...leaping in a procession.

The greater congregation in the clouds, multitudes in a procession of the many converted

Argo—Decan of Sartan

Argo Navis, Latin...*the ship*
Argo, Heb...*the company of travelers*
Shes en Fent, Copt, Egypt...*rejoicing over the serpent*
Al Safinah, Arabic...*a ship*
Ratis Heroum, Manlius...*heros's raft*
Nave Argo, Italian...*naval ship*
Pagasea Carina, *Ovid*
Argolico Puppis, Cicero...*travelers stern*
Schiff, German...*ship*

This sign has recently been divided into 3 by modern astronomers. Carina (the keel), Puppis (the stern), and Vela (the sail).

This was for modern astronomical convenience I suppose. The prophetic significance outweighs any modern convenience therefore I will not divide it into 3 constellations, but will reference the sections here in the whole.

This is 2/3rds of a ship, the sailors of the Pleiades (to sail), a meeting, and/ or arrival of saints preparing to return as shown in the next sign.

Alpha .4 white on tip of ship's 3rd oar as drawn (carina)

Suhail, Al Sahl, Arabic....trad. *beautiful, glorious, plain (clear) literal seems to suggest a knowledge (past) of imprisonment or persecution*
Kahi Nub, Coptic...*golden earth*
Subilon, unknown origin...*knowledge of past persecution*
Kabarnit, Assyrian... *shipmaster*
Karbana, Egyptian...*holders of the new beginning*
Soail Iamane, Greek...lit. *helpers of the persecuted*
Canobus, Canopus, Greek...*coming home through severe trouble*
Kanupus, Al Sufi-Arabic from Greek...*having increase, connected to the cross*
Yiedalion, Greek (Aratos, Hipparchos, Eudoxos)... *reaching beyond, delivered*

Beta 2.0 lower rear oar portion, keel (carina)

Miaplacidus, or Maia-placidus, Latin... *having to do with peace, contentment....Maia was the first named star in Pleiades*

Gamma 2, 6 and 8 white greenish white
and purple on front of vela-sail

Al Suheil al Muhlif, Arabic...*beauty of the oath, promise*
Al Muhlifain, Arabic...*the oath*

Delta 2.2 on bottom of sail (vela)

Koo She, Chinese...*arrows of heaven?*

Epsilon...on keel of ship center (carina) east of alpha

Avior, Arabic...*in sight (of Him)*

Zeta 2.5 east center of ship stern (puppis)

Naos, Burritts Atlas...*conflict seen*
Suhail Hadar, Al Sufi-Arabic...*knowing liberation is coming*

Eta irregular 1 to 7.4 reddish
Cluster in rear of stern (carina)

Tien She, China...*heavens altars*

Iota 2.9 pale yellow in stern?
(puppis?), or keel (carina) ?

Aspidiske, Ptolomy...*possession held firm*
Scutulum, Latin...*little shield*
Turais, Turyeish, Arabic-Al Tizini, -on the ornament of
the Apulstre...*focused ahead*

Kappa 3.9 in the stern (puppis) northern part front

Markeb, Markab, Arabic...*returning*

Lambda 2.5 in (vela) sail north front

Al Suheil al Wazn, Arabic...*weight of glory, beauty*

Phi 3.7 in the sail, (vela)

Tseen Ke, China...*heavens record*

A ship coming in. Heroes and travelers. Both seeing and being seen of Him who comes. Ships represent congregations, churches of believers. This ship is partly submerged but rising out of obscurity to prominence.

A ship with beautiful cargo, weight, glory; having seen persecution, rising up. Likely those added to the congregation in heaven during the tribulation. A company of travelers to be returning with the Lord.

Arieh, Hebrew/Leo, Latin

Arieh, Hebrew...*the lion rending*
Al Asad, Arabic...*the lion who rends*
Aryo, Syriac...*the lion who rends*
Pi-Mentekeon, Coptic...*plucking asunder*
Leon, Greek...*the lion*
Leo, Latin...Lowe, German...Leone, Italian...Leon, Spanish
Lyon, French... Leun, Angle-Norman...*the lion*
Sin, China...*lion*
Asleha, Sinha, Hindu....*lion*
Simham, Tamil...*lion*
Ser, Sher, Persian...*lion*

Alpha triple 1.7, 8.5, and 13 white and ultra-marine
on junction of right forearm and shoulder

Rex, Latin...*King*
Regulus, Latinized Hebrew...*the treading underfoot...King
of Justice*
Basiliskost, Ptolomy...*King s, or heavens slaughter*
Basiliskost Aster, Ptolomy...*King's " " " star*
Sharru, Mesopotamian, *the King*
Magha, India...*the Mighty*
Magh, Sogdiana...*the Great*
Miyan, Persia...*the Center*
Masu, Turanian (central Asia)...*the Hero*
Malikiyy, Arabic...*Kingly*
Basilica Stella, Latin...*Kings' star*
Al Kalb al Asad, Arabic...*the pursuit of the tearing lion*

Beta 2.3 blue on tip of lion's tail

Al Dhanab al Asad, Arabic...*trail of the tearer*
Denebola, Hebrew...*swift justice...swift Judge...coming
fast (Power known and seen)*
Al Aktab al Asad, Arabic-Kazwini...*the viscera of the lion
(renderer)*
Widhu, Widhayu, Sogdian, Korasmian...*the burning one*
Asphulia, Coptic...*wielding a terrible sword*
Aspholia, Greek-Kircher...*seeing His terrible sword*

Gamma double-binary, 2.2, 3.5
bright orange and greenish yellow on lions mane

Juba, Latin...*mane*
Al Jeb-bah, or Algeiba, likely Arabic for something
resembling *'fury'*...on the lion's mane

Delta coarsely triple 2.7, 13, and 9
Pale yellow, blue, and violet on rise of back, rear

Zosma, Zozma, Hebrew-Persian...*shining forth*
Al Thahr al Asad, Arabic-Ulug Beg...*the lions back*
Duhr, Dhur, unknown...lit. *deliverance begins*
Shang Seang, China...*High minister of state*
Armagh, Korasmian...*Great (with theta)*

Epsilon 3.3 yellow on tip of 'sickle' in lions head

Al Ras al Asad al Janubiyyah, Arabic...*the head of the lion -south*
Ta Tsze, China...*the Crown Prince*

Zeta double 3.7 and 6 middle of mane above gamma

Al Dhafara, Adhafera, Arabic...*putting down enemy*

Theta 3.5 on upper thigh rear leg below delta

Chort, unknown origin...*freeing prisoners*
Tsze Seang, China...*second Minister of state*
Al Haratan, Arabic, (with delta)...lit. *(prisoners) strength completely increased*

Iota binary, 4.6, and 7.4 yellowish-
below theta on rear leg

Tsze Tseang, China...*the second General*

Kappa double 4.8 and 10.5...yellow
and blue on nose of lion

Al Minchir al Asad, Arabic... *freed by the Renderer, (lion)*

Lambda 4.8 red on lion's mouth

Al Tarf, Arabic...*the unlimited power (of) King fixed*

Mu 4.3 orange between eyes and ears of lion on sickle

Al Ras al Asad al Shamaliyy, Arabic...*the head of the renderer going north*

Pi 5th magnitude just below Regulus under the lion

Yu Neu, China...*the honorable Lady*
(likely-Judah, Israel, believers congregation)

Xi 5th magnitude (with c, and d just below it)

Ling Tae, China...*a wonderful tower*
(likely-Jerusalem)

This is none other than the Lion of Judah. Y'shua, Yeshua, Issa, Iesu, Jesus, returning to devour the adversaries, and begin His Reign (Thy kingdom come).
What he comes to destroy is shown in the next sign.

Hydra—Decan of Arieh

Hydra, Hebrew...*the abhorred, serpent*
Hydre, French — Idra, Italian...*water snake, with meaning of thief in the camp, enemy within the borders, fraud, fake, enemy within*
Grosse Wasserschlange, German...*water snake abhorred*
Al Shuja, Arabic...*the snake*
Al Hayyah, Arabic—the snake...*lit. the tables turned on the separator*

El Havic, Semitic...*the fraudful disrupter*
Nile, Nahal, Egypt (see Beta Lepus)...Egyptians said to name their river from this grouping.

Alpha 2.0 orange lower front coil below head

Al Fard al Shuja, Arabic...*solitary one in the serpent (the separated)*
Al Unk al Shuja, Ulug Beg-Arabic...*the neck*
Al Fakar al Shuja, Arabic....*the backbone*
Cor Hydrae, Tycho...*the serpent's heart*
Kalb El havich, Kalbelaphard, Ricioli...*the hounding-pursuit of the serpent*
Al Drian, Arabic...*The abhorred*

Delta 4.6 on head of serpent

Al Minliar al Shuja, Ulug Beg-Arabic...*the nose of the serpent*
Minchir Alsugia, Arabic form...*the piercing of the deciever*
Min al Azal, Ulug Beg-Arabic...was for all the asterisms in the head *(unseen opposing(er) of truth)*

Tau 1, and 2 4.9 white, and 4.6 lilac, with iota and 5th mag. A in the coil below head

Ukdah, Kazwini...*the knot*
Kamph, Ptolomy...*much swearing, cursing, threats*

This is the kingdom of the antichrist, in the last moments of its return to prominence, which is considerably short, thankfully.

The provoker, subtle, liar, deceiver, imposter, curser, blasphemer in its death throes.

Al Arsh—Decan of Arieh

Al Arsh al Simak al Azal, Arabic...*the throne of the unarmed One*
Korax, Greek...*Raven*
Orebh, Orev, Hebrew...*the raven*
Eorosch, Avesta-Median...*raven*
Corvus, Latin...*the Raven*
Corvo, Corbean, Rabe...Italian, French, German...*crow, crow, and raven*

Alpha 4.3 orange on beak of raven

Al Minliar (minchir) al Ghurab, Arabic...*the beak of the raven, trad.*
piercing or tearing of the raven
Al Chibar, Arabic...*the seperated*
Chiba, Hebrew...*the curse, accursed*

Beta 3rd magnitude on claw, or foot of raven

Kraz, Semitic-unknown origin...*power to crush*

Gamma 2.3 on west upraised wing (right)

Gienah, unknown origin... *authority to imprison, execute?*
Al Janah al Ghurab al Aiman, Ulug Beg-Arabic...*the right wing of the raven*

Delta double 3.1 and 8.5 yellow and
purple- on east wing (left)

Algores, Proctor...*justice begins*
Algorab, Palermo calendar...*place of justice*

This is the end of the road for the unbelievers on earth. Judgment seat for those enemies of His return, and His people.

Crater—Decan of Arieh

Crater, unknown...*The cup*
Al Batinah, Al Achasi, Arabic....*a vessel*
Badiye, Persian...*vessel, cup*
Kalpeh, Kalp, Greek...*a cinerary urn*
Kantharoz, early Greek...*Goblet*
Urna, Roman...*Urn*
Poculum, Roman...*the cup*
Cratera, Cisero...*the cup*
Creter, ancient manuscripts...

> Alpha 4.1 orange on base of cup
> resting on serpents back

Al Kas, Arabic...*containing-having strength to crush (destroy)*
Alkes, Scalinger....*cup of judgment/destruction*
Alches, unknown...*delivering judgment*
Fundis vasis, Latin...*base of the vase*

Beta 4.4 magnitude lower left side of base of cup on serpent's back

Al Sharasif, Arabic...*the ribs (of the hydra)*
Ribs in scripture represent mankind, or nations. A bear was seen with 3 ribs in its mouth and it represented the kingdom of Persia, which was to devour much 'flesh'. See Daniel.

Destruction, judgment is poured out on the nations following the serpent (hydra).

Summary

The destroyed armies of the antichrist, babylon, and false prophet, their followers and minions now destroyed, the ravenous birds are invited in scripture to finish off the remains of those who came to destroy God's people, even the Messiah Himself. This represents the end of the war and the set-up of the throne of the unarmed one, now armed. Full circle. The Millenium Reign of Christ begins at the ending of this story.

From birth, The seed of the woman, The Branch, The Good Shepherd, His entry into Jeruasalem to pay the ransom, His death, crucifixion, burial, 3 days and nights in the heart of the earth, Resurrection, Ascension, Pentecost (Shavuot) Baptism, Church body grows, expands while persecuted-hated,... later Established, Valiant, Raptured, those that remain- Undermined, Surrounded, ...finally Delivered, seeing the return of the same Branch, now clearly the Lion of Judah, Good Shepherd, The Word of God, The Son of David to sit on the throne of His father David...and rule.

When you understand that the Word of God is replete with symbolic imagery or revelations, that those revelations were understood completely as coming from God and angels were usually interpreters, clarifying the meaning. These however have been in man's hands for millennia, and were so corrupted by myths and misunderstandings that God did not focus on them other than to mention them in passing in a few books, such as Psalms and Job, as well as part of the story of Jesus's birth. In fact astrologers and stargazers were missing the point of the story so often that the practice associated with the stars became synonomous with forbidden practices. However, there was more to the story, as I have attempted to convey here.

The story is near complete, the story logged down-written in the sky. It will remain a witness till all things are accomplished that were written down by the Prophets and Apostles....till a new heaven, and a new earth will be formed with wonders to be discovered as well, fresh and new.

A heavenly reminder of His plan for mankind written on the sky.

What an amazing discovery this was to me. Initially skeptical at seeing the title 'Gospel in the stars' by Joseph Seiss— having associated anything and everything with them to be astrology, something unreliable in the negative sense of the word. The charlatans and idol makers of old times and new, who misuse (d) the message in the names, misunderstood the pictures,... these speak of things they know nothing about selling to people who have no idea the meaning....yet those who understood found great treasure in them as prophetic signs...IE the wise men from the east, which in Jesus' time did still understand the prophetic timing of the motions and signals, with their meanings and found God's Son, the newborn King of Israel, to present Him gifts of royalty that could support the family in their flight to Egypt, or kept as a reminder of who they had as a Son.

Bible references per constellation

Bethulah/ The Virgin
Genesis 3:15; Amos 5:2; Isaiah 7:14, 11:1-2; Zechariah 3:8, 6:12; Matt 1-25; Luke 1:1-80; Revelation 12:1-2

Subilah-Coma/ Desired
Isaiah 9:6; Matt 1:24-25, 2:1-23; Luke 2:1-52

Bootes/The Shepherd
Job 9:9, 38:32; Psalm 23:1, 80:1; Isaiah 49 8-12; John 10:11-16; 1 Peter 2:25, 5:4

Kentaurus/-The Expiator
Isaiah 49:7, 53:3, 5; Zechariah 9:9; Matt 20:18-19, 21:1-11; Luke 22:20 John 12: 48

Mozanaim/ The Scales-purchase
Isaiah 53: 5, 10-11; Hosea 13:14; Zechariah 11:12-13; Matt 20: 28, 26:14-16; 1 Timothy 2:6

Adom/ Crux
Psalm 22:1-18; Matt 28:5; John 19:16-41; Luke 23:23, 33

Sura/ Lamb-sacrifice
Genesis 22:7-8; Exodus 12:1-11; Isaiah 53: 7; John 1:29,36; Revelation 5:6

Ataroth/ Crown -broken
Gen 49: 10; I Chronicles 20:2; Ezra 1:2; Luke 13:34-3519; John 18:36, 19:14-21

Akrabh/ Conflict
Isaiah 53: 8-9; Mark 15; John 12: 48-53, 18:6

Alyah/ Serpent
Genesis 3:1-4, 13-14; Revelation 12:15

Afeichus/ The Serpent Holder-treading upon
Matt 12:40, 27:51; Luke 23:47-56 ; 1 Peter 3:19-20, 4:6

Marsic/ The Bruiser-wounded in the foot
Genesis 3:15; Isaiah25: 7; Psalm 91:13; Isaiah 51:9

Kesheth/ The Archer-unconquered
Job 19:25; Isaiah: 25: 7-8; 26:19; Matt 27:52, 53; John 11:25; John 20

Lyra/ The Eagle-victorious
Matt 28:18; Luke 24: 51-53 ; John 20 :1-16

Ara/ Altar flames
Leviticus 6:9; Matt 27:51; Hebrews 9; Revelation 8:5

Thuban/ The Dragon-cast down
Isaiah 14:12, 27:1, 51:9; Luke 10:18; John 12: 31; Revelation 12:13

Gedi/ Life from death
Leviticus 16:8-9, 15-19; Isaiah 49:7; Luke 24:44

Sham/ Arrow
Psalm 144:6; Lamentations 3:12; Psalm 91:5

Neshr/ The Eagle-wounded
Exodus 19:4; Jeremiah 48:40; Ezekiel 1:10; Revelation 12: 14

Dalaph/ Water
Isaiah 12:1-3; John 1:4-5, 4:14; Luke 24:44-53

Deli/ The Outpouring
Isaiah 55:1; Joel 2:28-32; Luke 3:16; John 4:10, 7:38, 14:16-17, 26; Acts 2

Al Hut al Janubiyy/ Southern Fish
John 1:33, 7:38-39; Acts 2:4

Pekasus/ Swiftly Arriving
Psalms 143:10; Proverbs 1:23, Isaiah 61:1-3; John 14: 16,14:26; Acts 2:1-4

Azel/ The Swan-circling
Isaiah 52:7; Zechariah 4:6; Acts 2:6-47; Romans 10:15

Dagim/ Multiplying Fish
Matt 4:19, 24:14, 28:19-20; Luke 24: 46-48; Acts 2: 41-47, 16:5

Al Risha/ The Cord, or Way
Proverbs 12:28; John 14:5; Acts 16:6-13; Hebrews 10:20

Sirra/ The Chained
Acts 4:1-22, 4:29, 7: 51-60, 12:1-6; 1 Thessalonians 2:15-16

Kifaus/ The Counselor-Consoler
Psalms and Proverbs; Isaiah 9:6, 25:1; Jeremiah 31:10-14; The Gospels; 2 Corinthians 4:8-10; Revelation 3:21,22; Revelation 21

Taleh/ The Lamb
Matt 10:34, 16:18 ; Luke 22:36 ; John 18:36 ; Colossians 1:18 Revelation 5:6, 5:12, 12:11

Cassiopeia/ The Bride- making ready
Psalms 45:8; Ephesians 6:17; Revelation 2, Revelation 3

Kaitos/ Sea Beast
Daniel 7:1-8; Revelation 13:1-8, Revelation17

Perets/ The Breaker
Psalm 60:12, 198:13; Joel 3:10 ; Micah 2:13; Revelation 13: 3

Shor/ Aurochs-enraged bull
Deuteronomy 33:17; Job 38:31, 39:9-10; Isaiah 34:7; Revelation1: 20

K'sil/ Allied Warrior
Psalms 25:1-2, 60:11-12, 118:16; Daniel 11:32; Zechariah 9:13; 2 Corinth 2:14

Eridanus/ River of Judgment
Ezekiel 32:17-32; Matt 5:22; 2 Peter 2; Revelation 6:8

Aurignac/ The Driver
Psalm 35:17; Isaiah 43:14-21; Daniel 6:27

Thaumin/ The Twins
Isaiah 26:19; Daniel 12:2; Matt 25:1-13; 1 Corinthians 15:51-58; 1 Thessalonians 4:16-18

Arnebo/ Enemy of His Return
Daniel 8:23-25; Habakkuk 2:5-8; Revelation 12:13-17; Revelation 13

Abur/ The Mighty of the Right Hand
Isaiah 2:12-17; Revelation 7: 4-8; Revelation 11:3-13

Sebak/ Overcomers-once burdened
Revelation 7:9-14; 18:9; 1 John 5:4

Sartan/ Holding
Revelation 12:6; 13-17; Revelation 19:7-9; Matt 22:1-14

Arx/ The Lesser Bier-Procession
Jude 14; Revelation 18:7

Ash/ The Greater Bier- Procession
Matt 24:21; Revelation 12:11; Revelation 13:15

Argo/ Company of Travelers
Matt 8:11; 1 John 5:4; Revelation 2:26; 7:14

Arieh/ The Lion-vehement
Isaiah 26: 20-21; Revelation 5:5; Revelation 19:11-16;
Jude 14,15

Hydra/ The Water Serpent-worlds armies
Isaiah 27:1; Daniel 7: 23-25; Revelation 19: 19-21

Al Arsh/ The Throne
Daniel 7: 26; Revelation 19: 17-18

Crater/ Cup-judgment
Habakkuk 2:16; Revelation 19:20-21

Epilogue

This could be refined further, and further, to become clearer and clearer. The intent was to gather enough evidence together to come to a conclusion, and for myself that conclusion is that God named the stars, and has been telling the Gospel story from the sky since the beginning.

And as there may remain a very few names undefined or if the reader wishes...the tools are there for any who reads this to define any of the names, for further clarity, or confirmation....

This book *does not* replace the Word for guidance, inspiration, comfort, wisdom, or even understanding, in fact, my hope is that it will cause you the reader to crosscheck the story, with the written Word, which is eternal, pre-eminent, understanding there will be a new heaven and earth after all is accomplished in the prophecies of this age. The written Word has power, and by the same Word the heavens were created, and it is His Word that upholds this witness from millennia past...

From here with this basic understanding, the reader can add this witness to his/her arsenal of revelations, and can continue in study to the revealed Word of God in it's original form of Hebrew, and the Aleph-Bet. As stated, this is as illustrations of the revealed Word of God placed on the sky from antediluvian times, revealed to the prophets of old times.

Bibliography references

The King James Bible /James 1 of England 1602

Mysteries of the Alpha-Bet/ Marc Alain-Ouaknin 1999 c.

The Gospel in the Stars/Joseph A Seiss/ Kregel publications (recommended reading)

Mazzaroth, or The Constellations/ Frances Rolleston (recommended reading)

Star Names- Their Lore and Meaning/ Richard Hinckley Allen/Dover

Stars and Planets/ Jay Pasachoff/
Peterson Field Guides/Houghton-Mifflin

A Guide to Sky Watching/ David H. Levy/Fog city press

Some well known Astronomers

Al Achasi - Egyptian astronomer of Cairo Cir. 1650 AD. Sheik and Muslim teacher.

Al Sufi - Azofi, or Abd al Rahman al Sufi....Persian astronomer 964 AD compiled 'Book of fixed stars' based on Ptolomy's work.

Abu Masher-Albumazer- Arab astronomer to Caliphs of Grenada (Spain) Cir. 800 AD. Considered Persian astronomy accurate, and Indian tables mixed and changed.

Aben Ezra- Rabbi contemporary with Abu-Masher.

Aratos- Stoi (stoic) philosopher-astronomer of Soloi. Greek. Cir. 310-245 BC

Bayer-Johann Bayer, German astronomer Cir. 1600 AD catalogued stars in constellations with small case Greek designations, combined with Latin designations of constellations. EG. Beta-Tauri.

Beigh- (Ulug Beg), Tartar astronomer Cir. 1450 AD. Grandson of Tamerlane.

Burritt-E.H Burritt, his atlas in 1835 designed to illustrate the geography of the heavens.

Cassini-Giovanni Cassini 1625-1712...Jesuit Astronomer of Genoa, (Italy).

Cicero- Roman orator and philosopher, lawyer, and statesman, considered one of Rome's best orators. Cir 104-43 BC.

Copernicus-15th century Polish astronomer discovering a sun centered, not earth centered sky.

Caesar Germanicus-nephew and adopted son of Emperor Tiberius (AD 14-37) Immensely popular general.

Flamsteed-Astronomer of early 18th century assigned number to any given star of a constellation based on its order of right ascension. Flamsteed's catalogue 1725.

Hipparchos-Greek astronomer, founder of trigonometry Cir. 190-120 BC. Nicea, Asia Minor.

Hyde-Published Hyde's -syntaxis 1660 using Ulug Beg's catalogue.

Kazwini-Abu Yaha Zakariya Ibn Multanid (?) Al Qazwini, Persian physician and astronomer Cir. 1280 AD. Wrote 'marvels of creatures and strange things existing'. A cosmology in Arabic.

Nonnus- Greek epic poet of 4th-early 5th century AD. Converted to Christianity.

Pliny (the elder)-Roman author car 23-79AD Pliny the younger was avid persecutor of Christianity.

Ptolemy-Claudius Ptolemy, Roman citizen of Egypt AD 90- 168. Mathematician, astronomer, geographer, wrote the Almagest...an astronomical treatise....possibly an astrologer (misuse of signs).

Riccioli-Italian astronomer and astronomical writer Cir. 1598. Wrote Almagestum Novum. Opposed sun centered system.

Vetruvius- Roman writer, architect, military commander, 1st century AD.